VEGAN
ON THE GO

Fast, easy, affordable—
anytime, anywhere

Jérôme Eckmeier | Daniela Lais

VEGAN
ON THE GO

Fast, easy, affordable—
anytime, anywhere

With photography by Brigitte Sporrer

CONTENTS

16 SNACKS & SMALL BITES

snacks between meals—smoothies, finger food, etc.

44 SOUPS & SALADS

creamy soups, stews, & salads from all over the world

84 SANDWICHES, WRAPS, & ROLLS

from sandwiches to burgers—spreads, toppings, & wraps

122 SATISFYING MAINS

hearty & filling—vegetables, pasta, & rice

162 SOMETHING SWEET

quick treats—creamy desserts, cakes, & pastries

INTRODUCTION

Even on hectic days, your stomach will be rumbling by lunchtime. But your phone rings and there's an email to send before you can quickly find something to eat… and in no time at all, your lunch break is over. Sound familiar?

We'd all like our midday meal to be healthy and with plenty of fresh fruit and vegetables. But, in the real world, our good intentions are often sabotaged by a lack of time, and we end up back at the uninspiring snack bar around the corner.

If you're looking for something vegan, you might get lucky even there. More and more often these days, cafés are offering vegan snacks. This is a great improvement. But still, sometimes you end up having to go on a food hunt. And let's be honest: often what you can find is pretty far removed from a balanced meal.

No wonder that full- and part-time vegetarians prefer to bring their own food from home. In a survey of 3,500 vegetarians, 75 percent packed their own lunch several times each week. The kinds of recipes they want are balanced, simple, and quick. And that is exactly what you will find in this book. Here are plenty of vegan ideas for lunch box classics such as colorful sandwiches and cold dishes—which our survey respondents put right at the top of their list—as well as soups and warm dishes that can easily be reheated at the office and guarantee a delicious and stress-free lunch break.

And if you are wondering when you might have time to prepare these meals, I have a tip for you: every so often, meet up with family or friends on a Sunday for a communal cooking session. Together you'll have so much more fun chopping, sizzling, and baking than you would on your own and, by the end, your fridge will be bursting with plant-based delicacies for your own completely personalized lunch box.

Yours, Sebastian Joy
Managing Director of the German Vegetarian Society

PACKING WELL

A huge variety of lunch boxes are available. Choose one that is strong and airtight, so that nothing can leak out. Buy yourself a large, medium, and small box made from stainless steel, recycled plastic, or renewable raw materials, and get an insulated container for soups or warm dishes and a vacuum flask for smoothies or other drinks—these will usually keep your lunch warm for up to 6 hours, or cool for up to 24 hours. Practical alternatives include thoroughly cleaned, recycled plastic containers with a tight-fitting lid, screw-top jars, or preserving jars, as well as foil and plastic wrap. Dressings are best transported separately, possibly in a spare compartment in your lunch box, or in a little glass jar.

Many offices are equipped with a small kitchen, including a microwave or stove for reheating, so using a microwaveable, or heat-resistant, container saves you from dumping your lunch onto a plate, thus creating extra dishwashing. Unless it is in an insulated container, food should always be kept in a cool place, so get yourself a little corner of the office fridge and kitchen cabinets to store your food and seasonings.

VEGAN BASICS— THE PANTRY

If you keep some basics in your pantry, you will only need to purchase a few additional fresh ingredients each week, and getting your lunch box ready will be as easy as pie. Our recipes have been kept nice and simple, and the ingredients are not hard to obtain. Most can be found in a well-stocked supermarket and, if not there, then at a health food store, organic store, pharmacy, or vegan mail-order company.

IN THE FREEZER

Fresh vegetables cleaned, blanched if necessary, and stored in portions, keep for several months.

Frozen vegetables usually contain more vitamins than fresh vegetables, since they are frozen immediately after harvesting. Pay attention to the producer's best-before dates.

Lemon juice and **sauces** in little portions for dressings, sauces, or for flavoring; keep for a few weeks.

Pastry and dough: pizza dough, puff pastry, pie crust, and filo (homemade or store-bought) will keep for a few months in the freezer.

(continued on page 10)

IN THE FRIDGE

Fresh **herbs** will keep in the fridge for up to 1 week, wrapped in damp paper towels.

Vegan **margarine** should keep in the fridge for at least 3 weeks.

Nondairy milk such as soy, rice, oat, almond, nut, or multigrain milks and drinks. For spicy dishes, use a sugar-free vegetable milk; for baking, use soy milk because it thickens in combination with vinegar and combines well with other ingredients. Unopened, it can be kept without chilling for several months; once opened, store in the fridge and use within 3–4 days.

Unopened soy, oat, or rice cream can be stored at room temperature for at least 6 months; once opened, store in the fridge and use within 2–3 days.

Soy yogurt without added sugar will keep in the fridge for around 2 weeks.

Unopened tempeh can be stored without chilling for several months; once opened, it will keep in the fridge for up to 8 weeks, but must then be used without further delay.

Tofu: natural tofu (with no added flavors) and / or smoked tofu (already seasoned) will both keep unopened in the fridge for at least 2 weeks. Natural tofu stored in brine should be kept in a covered container, with the brine always covering the tofu.

Tomato purée will keep unopened and protected from the light for at least a few months; once opened, store in the fridge and use it up within 1–2 weeks.

IN THE PANTRY

Cans of vegetables, pulses, and fruits.

Preserves in jars such as pickles, olives, tomatoes, and peppers.

Dried fruits and vegetables such as mushrooms, tomatoes, and chiles.

Herbs and spices (dried): among the most useful are chili powder, curry powder, garam masala, smoked paprika, ginger, cumin, herbes de Provençe, turmeric, marjoram, nutmeg, oregano, paprika, pepper, allspice, salt, and cinnamon.

Yeast flakes for seasoning and to create a "cheesy" flavor (see p94 and p158).

Olive oil, ideally cold-pressed, good-quality organic.

Flours for baking, binding, and thickening, such as plain flour and chickpea flour.

Nuts and seeds: it's a good idea to keep chia seeds, cashews, hazelnuts, sesame seeds, and walnuts.

Pasta is an essential, as a basis for so many dishes.

Quinoa, rice, or wild rice can also form the basis for lots of salads, side dishes, and fillings.

Textured soy or TVP (textured vegetable protein), finely or coarsely ground, diced, or as a steak.

Seasoning and sweeteners such as agave syrup, maple syrup, barbecue sauce, vinegar, vegetable stock or bouillon, tomato ketchup, soy sauce, miso, and tahini.

LIGHTNING-QUICK LUNCH BOX RECIPES

Sometimes you just need something super-quick to grab in the morning when you're trying to pack up your lunch or snack. The perfect thing is having leftovers from the previous day that you can just throw into a lunch box, so try to cook more than you need for your evening meal. But even if you don't have leftovers to help you out, there are lots of other options.

Filled rolls or bread with toppings are particularly quick—just add in a few vegetable sticks. If you get hungry between meals, nuts are perfect. The best thing is to put together your own nut mixture, which you can then perk up with chocolate chips or whatever else you like. A fresh fruit salad is also easy to assemble—add a dash of lemon juice to prevent the fruit from turning brown. And maybe you can treat yourself to something to nibble on—vegan nachos, chips, and pretzels don't have to be just for watching television! Try some delicious dips to go with them (see p30, pp56–57, pp90–94, and p106).

MORNING MUESLI

Often there isn't even enough time for breakfast in the morning—and that's when muesli is the perfect thing to take with you on the go. Muesli is simple to make vegan by using soy yogurt or a nondairy milk. You can buy ready-made muesli mixtures, or assemble a batch yourself, depending on what grains, nuts, fruits, and seeds you like. With some protein-rich chia seeds added, it can become a real power food.

Muesli with chia seeds and fruit

Peel **1 tangerine** and split into segments, slice up **1 small banana**, and chop **½ apple**. Mix the fruit with **½ cup (150g) soy yogurt**, **1 tbsp fine oat bran**, and **1 tsp chia seeds**. Sweeten with **2 tbsp agave syrup**.

Overnight oats

The evening before, put **1/2 cup (50g) fine oat bran** into a jar with a screw-top lid. Add **1 cup (240ml) hot water** and **¾oz (20g) frozen raspberries** and leave to soak overnight. The next morning, stir in **2 tbsp agave syrup** and **1 tbsp chopped cashews** (or other nuts).

SPREADS FOR YOUR BREAD: THE BASICS

Bread is the ultimate quick lunch box savior! These days, stores sell plenty of vegan spreads, but homemade spreads have the advantage that they can be varied to suit your own taste. Make spreads from pulses, nuts, seeds, vegetables, fruit, rice or rice cakes, and silken or smoked tofu. Add fresh or dried herbs and spices to enhance the flavors. Be creative and stock up on delicious ingredients, which will save you time every morning. You will find more spread recipes in the book, too (see pp90–94).

Basic sunflower seed spread

Toast **¾ cup (100g) sunflower seeds** in a pan without any oil. Put them in a food processor and grind, gradually adding **6–8 tbsp sunflower oil**. If desired, add a splash of water or lemon juice. Spice it up with dried **herbs, salt, pepper, and smoked paprika,** or just eat as it is with a bit of jam on your bread. The savory version also works wonderfully as a dip.

QUICK SOUPS

Especially in winter, soups are a welcome and warming meal. If you have a microwave or a stove at work, you can pretty much take your own supplies with a jar of tomato purée and/or instant vegetable stock, soup noodles, and some croutons. For a simple broth with croutons, you can use hot water from the coffeemaker. You'll find more delicious soup recipes later (see pp44–53).

Alphabet spaghetti soup

Heat **1 tbsp oil** in a saucepan, finely slice a **small piece of leek** into rings and sauté briefly, then add **1¼ cups (300ml) water** and **½ vegetable stock cube** and bring to a boil. As soon as the water is boiling, add **½ cup (80g) alphabet pasta** and cook according to package instructions (around 6–7 minutes). Pour into a bowl and sprinkle with **1 tsp chopped parsley**, if desired.

Tomato soup

Finely chop **½ cup (70g) mixed vegetables** (carrots, celery, leek). Heat **1 tbsp oil** in a saucepan, lightly brown the vegetables, add **1½ cup (300ml) tomato purée**, and thin with a little vegetable stock or water, then simmer for a few minutes until the vegetables are just cooked. Season with salt and pepper and, if desired, stir in **1 tbsp fresh or frozen herbs** and **1 tbsp** vegan cream.

QUICK AND HEALTHY SALADS

Salads are ideal for the vegan lunch box. The basic ingredients are usually vegan anyway, they are a great way to use up leftover fruit and vegetables that you have at home, and are usually quick to prepare. Here are a couple of suggestions, but go ahead and make up your own creations, or find more salad recipes later in the book (see pp60–83).

Turbo tabbouleh

Bring **3 tbsp couscous** to a boil with double that quantity of **salted water**. Turn off the stove, cover, and leave to steep for 10 minutes. In the meantime, wash and finely chop **4 cherry tomatoes, ½ zucchini, 6 mint leaves,** and **6 sprigs of parsley**. Mix together a citrus dressing using the juice of **1 lime, 3 tbsp olive oil, salt,** and plenty of **black pepper**. Mix all the ingredients well.

Speedy sprouting salad

Mix **2 handfuls** of your chosen **bean sprouts** (homegrown or bought) with **1 handful of seasonal lettuce leaves** and **1 orange**, split into segments. Blend **2 tbsp oil** and **2 tbsp vinegar** with the juice you retained from the **orange** and add this to the **salad**. Mix everything thoroughly and season to taste with **salt** and ground **mixed colored peppercorns**.

Smoked tofu salad

Wash, dry, and roughly shred **2–3 handfuls of seasonal lettuce leaves**. Finely chop some leftover vegetables (**pepper, cucumber, olives**) and fold these in. Mix with a dressing made from **1 tbsp cider vinegar, 3 tbsp olive oil, salt, pepper,** and a **squeeze of lemon juice**. Chop **3½oz (100g) smoked tofu** into cubes, sauté in **1 tbsp olive oil** over high heat, and then add a **dash of soy sauce**. Fold into the salad along with **1 tbsp sesame seeds**.

Vegan sausage salad

Slice **5½oz (150g) vegan sausage, 4 pickles,** and **3 radishes**. Peel, halve, and slice **1 small red onion** into fine rings. Halve and seed **1 small pepper** and finely chop. Whisk **2 tbsp oil** with **1 tbsp vinegar** and **1 tsp mustard**, pour it over the other ingredients, mix everything together, and season to taste with **salt** and **pepper**. If desired, garnish with **2 tbsp watercress**.

VEGAN FOOD IN RESTAURANTS

Even with the very best intentions, it's just not always possible take a lunch box with you. And social reasons, too, will mean that now and then you'll end up eating at a restaurant. Here's a quick look at what your vegan options might be in different venues.

Italian

Italian restaurants are often really flexible and great places to go for vegan food. Pizza dough is generally vegan, although it's always best to ask. Order a pizza topped (generously) with just tomato sauce and vegetables and then refine it however you like, with garlic or chili oil. Lots of Italian restaurants also have pasta made without egg. The best sauce options are tomato sauce or just *aglio e olio*. Sadly, you should avoid gnocchi, as they are usually a ready-made product that contains milk powder, or eggs, or other dairy products.

Indian

Here it's always important to ask about ghee (clarified butter), which is included in a great deal of dishes. Dhals are usually vegan, provided that no ghee has been added. *Aloo gobi* (potatoes and cauliflower in a spicy sauce) is a standard recipe at many Indian restaurants and is nearly always vegan. Lots of pakora recipes (a fried dish made with a chickpea flour batter) can also be made without any animal products. The papadums ordered as a side dish are always vegan, likewise roti. Unfortunately, ghee is often used in naan breads.

Mexican

You can order tacos filled with vegetables at every Mexican restaurant. For the sauce, stick to the sharp, red sauces as they just use tomatoes as their basic ingredient. Enchiladas can also usually be made vegan, and are a good lunchtime snack.

Chinese

There is a Buddhist fasting dish made with tofu and bean sprouts that is on the menu at virtually every Chinese restaurant and is always vegan. Vegetables with fried rice are also often available; just make sure that you order them without egg. The traditional miso soup is also vegan. When ordering Asian food, it is important to mention that you don't want any fish sauce added to the dish. In terms of dessert, the baked fruits are usually vegan, as long as you order them without honey, of course.

Fast-food restaurants

You can't go wrong with falafel here. These round balls made from chickpeas are always vegan, stuffed into pita bread with all kinds of vegetables, and make a filling meal. Things are a bit trickier when it comes to the sauce, as these are usually made from yogurt or dairy products. The best option is to ask for a plain tahini sauce, that has not been mixed with yogurt.

Modern American food

The biggest challenge often comes at traditional American restaurants. Vegetable dishes are nearly always available, but make sure that the vegetables have not been tossed in butter. You can also order salads with vinaigrette made from oil and vinegar. Otherwise, the best thing is to call the restaurant in advance and explicitly ask for vegan food—demand influences supply, and the more often vegan dishes are requested, the sooner restaurants will begin to adjust!

SNACKS & SMALL BITES

snacks between meals—smoothies,
finger food, etc.

MUESLI BARS

Dried fruits and nuts give you ample fuel for the day ahead, while amaranth provides calcium, magnesium, iron, and zinc. Muesli bars are the perfect morning snack, a source of power in your lunch box. They are quick to prepare and these sweet bars, with their hearty oat flakes, have everything you could want from a quick energy boost. You can vary the dried fruits as you like, as long as you use the same quantity, so the recipe will never get boring.

1¾oz (50g) macadamia nuts
1¾oz (50g) hazelnuts
1¾oz (50g) cashews
9oz (250g) dried fruit (raisins, dates, goji berries, apricots)
5 tbsp vegan margarine
5 tbsp demerara sugar
¾ cup (150ml) agave syrup
2 tbsp lemon juice
1oz (30g) puffed amaranth
1¼ cups (200g) jumbo oats
pinch of ground cinnamon

1 Preheat the oven to 350°F (180°C). Roughly chop all the nuts with a knife or in a food processor. Depending on the variety, either leave the dried fruit whole or chop it into little pieces.

2 Put the margarine, sugar, and agave syrup into a saucepan and bring to a boil over high heat. Stir in the nuts, dried fruit, lemon juice, puffed amaranth, oats, and cinnamon.

3 Line a baking sheet with parchment paper. Use a moistened spatula to spread the mixture over the sheet in a ¾in (2cm) thick layer. Bake in the center of the oven for around 15 minutes until the mixture is holding together well. Slice into 12 bars while still warm, then leave to cool and store in an airtight container.

TIP

A large green smoothie provides
you with vitamins and energy
for the whole day.

SPINACH AND BANANA SMOOTHIE

Peel the banana and the orange and coarsely chop. Peel the apple, cut into quarters, remove the core, and chop roughly. Add all the fruit chunks and the spinach to a food processer. Peel and finely grate the ginger and add to the food processor with the lemon juice, baobab and moringa powders (if using), and linseed oil. Blend the ingredients until smooth, then pour in 16fl oz (500ml) water and mix everything briefly once again. Decant into little bottles and chill for 1–2 hours. Or you can chill it in a vacuum flask and serve 1 portion at a time.

1 very ripe banana
1 small orange
1 small apple
2½ cups (75g) baby spinach
½in (1.5cm) piece of fresh ginger
juice of 1 small lemon
1 tbsp baobab powder (optional;
 from a health food store
 or online)
1 tsp moringa powder (optional;
 from a health food store
 or online)
½ tsp linseed oil

ALMOND AND CINNAMON DRINK

Whisk all the ingredients vigorously, either by hand in a bowl using a balloon whisk, or put them into a food processor and mix briefly. Pour the drink into little bottles and chill for 1–2 hours. Or you can chill it in a vacuum flask and serve 1 portion at a time.

Makes 2 glasses
Preparation: 5 minutes
+ 1–2 hours chilling time

2 cups (500ml) almond milk,
 or other plant-based milk
1 tbsp apple syrup
pinch of ground star anise
pinch of salt
pinch of ground cardamom
1 tsp ground cinnamon

PESTO AND "RICOTTA" BALLS

So simple, so delicious: these have a fresh edge that will enhance any lunch box. They are also great to serve at a party, and can be put into a pretty glass to take along as a gift for your hosts.

4 cups (1 liter) soy milk
5 tbsp cider vinegar
bunch of Thai basil
5 tsp vegan basil pesto
½ tsp chili powder
sea salt
freshly ground black pepper
olive oil, for marinating

1 Bring the soy milk to a boil in a pan over high heat. As soon as it begins to boil, stir in the vinegar. Remove the pan from the heat and leave the mixture to cool—during this time, the solid components will settle. Carefully pour away the liquid. Put the remaining solid ingredients into a strainer lined with a clean kitchen towel. Bring the corners of the towel together and then twist, so that as much liquid as possible is squeezed out.

2 Pull the leaves from the basil and chop them roughly. Mix together the soy "ricotta" in a bowl with the pesto and chili powder and season to taste with salt and pepper. Form 10 little balls from the mixture and put them in a screw-top jar or preserving jar with the basil leaves. Completely cover with the oil and leave to infuse for 3–4 days.

TIP

```
If you can, leave the jar in the fridge in
your office kitchen and just help yourself
whenever you like. These are great with
salad, or bread, or layered up with sliced
tomatoes in a lunch box.
```

LITTLE POTATO CAKES
WITH YOGURT DIP

These delicious bites can be fried, or baked in the oven without any oil at all. Serve with this fresh yogurt dip, flavored with a few chives. It's a little snack to pep you up and that you can enjoy with a completely clear conscience.

1 Peel the potatoes, cut into large chunks, and boil in salted water for around 15 minutes until soft. Drain and transfer to a bowl. While still warm, mash with a fork until fairly smooth. Add the flour, 1 tsp more salt, and the herbes de Provençe, and work everything together to a smooth consistency.

2 Roll out the mix until it is ¼in (5mm) thick on a generously floured work surface, using a rolling pin that you have also liberally coated with flour. Dust a 2½in (6cm) diameter round cutter or glass with flour and cut out discs. Heat the oil in a pan and fry the potato cakes on both sides until golden brown. Remove and drain on paper towels, then leave to cool.

3 To make the dip, stir together the yogurt and chives and season to taste with salt and pepper. Pack up the potato cakes and the dip separately to take with you.

For the cakes
7oz (200g) waxy potatoes
sea salt
1 cup (120g) white spelt flour, plus extra for dusting
2 tsp herbes de Provençe
1–2 tbsp oil

For the dip
3–4 tbsp soy yogurt, or other plant-based yogurt
1 tbsp chopped chives
sea salt
freshly ground black pepper

TIP

```
The potato cakes can also be baked in the
oven. Preheat the oven to 350°F (180°C),
place them on a baking sheet lined with
parchment paper, and prick each several
times with a fork. Bake in the center of the
oven for 10 minutes, then turn them over and
bake for a further 10 minutes, or until they
are a pale golden brown color.
```

Makes 2 snack portions
Preparation: 10 minutes
+ 25 minutes cooking time

¾ cup (200g) canned chickpeas
    (drained weight)
2 tbsp olive oil
2 tsp garam masala
1 tsp sea salt
1 tsp onion powder

ROASTED CHICKPEAS

1 Preheat the oven to 400°F (200°C). Drain the chickpeas, carefully pat them dry with a kitchen towel, and transfer them to a bowl. Add the oil, garam masala, salt, and onion powder and gently mix with your hands until the oil and spices are evenly distributed.

2 Line a baking sheet with parchment paper and spread the chickpeas over it so they lie in a single layer. Bake in the center of the oven for 10 minutes, then turn. Increase the oven temperature to 425°F (220°C) and bake for a further 10–13 minutes. Leave to cool completely and they will crisp up.

Makes 2 snack portions
Preparation: 10 minutes
+ 30 minutes cooking time

½ cauliflower, about 1lb 2oz (500g)
1 tbsp chili oil
2 tbsp olive oil
pinch of chili powder
2 tsp mild curry powder
pinch of ground allspice
½ tsp ground cumin
pinch of ground turmeric
3 slightly heaped tsp Thai
    chili paste

SPICY OVEN-ROASTED CAULIFLOWER

1 Preheat the oven to 375°F (190°C). Split the cauliflower into florets and place in a bowl. Line a baking sheet with parchment paper. Put both types of oil into a screw-top jar along with all the spices and the chili paste. Close the lid and shake the jar vigorously until the ingredients combine to make a smooth paste.

2 Use your hands or a pastry brush to distribute the spicy paste all over the cauliflower florets. Spread the cauliflower over the baking sheet and bake in the center of the oven for 25–30 minutes. Use a toothpick to test whether it is cooked; it should pass through a floret with no resistance. The cauliflower is delicious warm or cold.

SPICY KALE CHIPS

Makes 1–2 snack portions
Preparation: 10 minutes
+ 15 minutes cooking time

1 Preheat the oven to 340°F (170°C). Line a baking sheet with parchment paper. Wash the kale and dry it thoroughly, then remove and discard any coarse stalks. Shred the leaves into large pieces. Mix the oil and soy sauce in a small bowl. Brush the kale leaves on both sides with the oil mixture and lay them on the baking sheet. The leaves should not overlap, so if necessary bake in batches.

2 Mix the chili powder and yeast flakes in another small bowl and sprinkle over the kale leaves. Depending on their thickness, bake in the center of the oven for around 15 minutes until crisp. Remove and leave to cool completely.

2½ cups (175g) curly kale, chopped
1 tbsp sesame oil
½ tsp soy sauce
pinch of chili powder
pinch of yeast flakes

SMOKY COCONUT "BACON"

Makes 2 snack portions
Preparation: 10 minutes
+ 20 minutes cooking time

1 Preheat the oven to 275°F (140°C). Put the coconut chips into a bowl. Whisk together the maple syrup, soy sauce, liquid smoke, and 1 tsp of water. Pour this over the coconut chips and gently mix everything with your hands until the liquid is evenly distributed. Sprinkle over the paprika and mix it in.

2 Line a baking sheet with parchment paper and spread the coconut chips on it; they should not be overlapping. Bake in the center of the oven for 15–20 minutes, turning 2–3 times during cooking. Remove and leave to cool completely.

1½ cups (125g) coconut chips
1 tbsp maple syrup
1 tbsp soy sauce
1 tsp liquid smoke (optional; from a delicatessen or online)
½ tsp smoked paprika

TIP

The kale chips can be eaten as a little nibble, but they also work wonderfully as a topping on a sandwich or burger.

Makes 2–3 snack portions
Preparation: 10 minutes

2 ripe avocados (ideally, the
    Hass variety)
½ red chile
1 small green chile
1 garlic clove (optional)
juice and zest of ½ unwaxed lime
½ tsp sea salt
pinch of freshly ground white
    pepper

To serve
vegetable sticks (such as peppers,
    carrots, or celery)
vegan tortilla chips or crackers

GUACAMOLE

1 Halve the avocados and remove the pits. Scrape out the flesh
from the skins with a spoon, put it into a small bowl, and mash
with a fork. Seed the red chile and finely chop. Slice the green chile
into little rings. Peel the garlic (if using) and either chop very finely
or crush in a garlic press.

2 Add the red chile, garlic, lime juice, and zest to the avocado.
Stir well and season to taste with salt and pepper. Decorate with
green chile rings. Then take along whatever you like dipping in it:
vegetable sticks, tortilla chips, or crackers.

Makes 2 snack portions
Preparation: 10 minutes
+ 24 hours soaking time
+ 1 hour cooking time

½ cup (125g) dried chickpeas
sea salt
1 garlic clove
1 tbsp lemon juice
1 tbsp tahini
pinch of paprika, plus extra
    to serve
freshly ground black pepper
4 tbsp olive oil, plus extra to serve

HUMMUS

1 Leave the chickpeas to soak, covered in water, for 24 hours.
Drain and put them into a pan, cover with slightly salted water,
and simmer with the lid on over low heat for around 1 hour, until they
are soft. Drain in a strainer. Peel and crush the garlic.

2 Put the chickpeas into a blender with the garlic, lemon juice,
tahini, ½ tsp more salt, the paprika, and some pepper and purée
until smooth. Gradually add enough oil to make a smooth, velvety
consistency. Put the hummus into a lunch box. Use a spoon to draw
a spiral in the surface, drizzle on a little more oil, and garnish with
paprika. This goes well with flatbreads.

```
TIP    Soaked, freshly cooked chickpeas
       have a better flavor and firmer
       consistency than the canned
       variety. But if you're in a hurry,
       feel free to use canned chickpeas;
       you will need double the quantity.
```

Makes 2–3 snack portions
Preparation: 15 minutes
+ 30 minutes cooking time

CARROT HEART SUSHI

1 Wash the rice in a strainer under cold running water until the water runs clear. Let it drain thoroughly. Transfer to a saucepan, cover with cold water, bring to a boil, cover, and simmer over low heat for around 15 minutes. Turn off the heat and leave the rice to swell for a further 15 minutes.

2 Meanwhile, peel the carrots. Along both sides of the length of the carrots, cut down toward a central point so that each carrot is teardrop shaped. Now, along the curved broad edges, cut a notch centrally down the length of each carrot. Finally, on each side, carve out a curve. You are aiming to sculpt carrots whose cross-sections are heart-shaped. Cook the carrots in a pan of salted water for 5–10 minutes, until al dente.

3 Mix together the vinegar with the syrup or sugar and ¾ tsp salt. Mix this sweetened vinegar with the still-warm rice, then leave it to cool. Let the carrots drain, then pat them dry.

4 Lay out 1 nori sheet on a bamboo mat. With moistened fingers, spread out half of the rice on the sheet, leaving a ¾in (2cm) border along the upper edge. Lay 1 carrot on the lower edge and carefully roll up the sheet. Brush the bare strip of nori with water and press it down. Follow the same process with the second sheet of nori and the remaining rice and carrot. Slice the rolls into pieces using a very sharp, dampened knife and sprinkle with sesame seeds (if using). Pack up the sushi, soy sauce, wasabi, and ginger separately to take with you.

For the sushi rolls
½ cup (125g) sushi rice
2 carrots
sea salt
1½ tbsp rice vinegar
1½ tsp rice syrup, or sugar
2 nori sheets (see Tip, below)
toasted sesame seeds, for
   sprinkling (optional)

To serve
soy sauce
wasabi
pickled sushi ginger

Special equipment
bamboo mat, for rolling (from an
   Asian grocery store)

TIP You can buy sheets of nori in various sizes. The length of your carrots should correspond to the size of the nori sheet. If you'd like a bit more umami flavor, cook the carrots the day before and marinate them overnight in soy sauce. Pat dry before using.

Makes 3–4 snack portions
Preparation: 35 minutes
+ 30 minutes cooking time

SMOKED TOFU AND CRUNCHY VEGGIE SUSHI

Asian dishes are particularly well suited to the lunch box. Here we roll up some cucumber, parsnip, smoked tofu, and avocado, with wasabi paste giving an astringent kick. It's practical for transporting, eating, and dipping. And, best of all, it's good for you!

For the sushi rolls
½ cup (125g) sushi rice
¼ cucumber
1 small parsnip
1¾oz (50g) smoked tofu
¼ avocado
2½ tsp rice vinegar
½ tbsp granulated sugar
¼ tsp sea salt
½ tbsp canola oil
½ tbsp soy sauce
3 nori sheets
wasabi paste

To serve
soy sauce
sweet chili sauce

Special equipment
bamboo mat, for rolling (from an
   Asian grocery store)

1 Wash the rice in a strainer under cold running water until the water runs clear. Let it drain thoroughly. Transfer to a saucepan, cover with cold water, bring to a boil, cover, and simmer over low heat for around 15 minutes. Turn off the heat and leave the rice to swell for a further 15 minutes.

2 Meanwhile, peel the cucumber and parsnip and slice into even, thin strips. Slice the smoked tofu into thin strips. Carefully scoop out the flesh of the avocado from the skin with a spoon in a single piece and slice into strips.

3 Stir together the vinegar, sugar, and salt in a bowl. Mix this sweetened vinegar with the still-warm rice, then leave it to cool. Heat the oil in a pan and briefly brown the smoked tofu and parsnip over medium heat. Add the soy sauce.

4 Lay out 1 nori sheet on a bamboo mat. Spread out half the rice so that it is around ¼in (5mm) thick and make a dip along the center with your thumb. Put a little wasabi paste into the lower half of the dip. Fill the entire dip evenly with half the cucumber, parsnip, smoked tofu, and avocado. Carefully roll it up, press gently together, and brush with a bit of water. Do the same with the second nori sheet and the remaining fillings. Slice the rolls into pieces using a very sharp, dampened knife. Package up the little sushi rolls and the dipping sauces separately to take along with you.

Makes 2–3 snack portions
(5 rolls)
Preparation: 30 minutes
+ 12 hours marinating time

SOBA NOODLE SUMMER ROLLS
WITH TOFU AND CILANTRO

1 Drain the tofu and dry it thoroughly using paper towels. Cut into sticks and lay in a flat dish. Stir together the curry paste and orange juice in a small bowl. Pour evenly over the tofu sticks, cover, and leave to marinate in the fridge for 12 hours. Let the tofu drain thoroughly. Heat the oil in a pan and brown the sticks on all sides over high heat. Drain on some paper towels and season well with salt and pepper. Leave to cool.

2 In the meantime, boil the soba noodles for 6 minutes in salted water, or according to the package instructions, then drain in a strainer and plunge into cold water to stop the cooking. Drain again. Peel the cucumber and carrot and slice into fine sticks. Pick the leaves from the cilantro.

3 In a flat dish, leave 1 spring roll wrapper to soak for 1–2 minutes in very warm water. Carefully spread this out on a clean work surface. Spread one-fifth of the vegetables centrally across the sheet, top this with one-fifth of the soba noodles and finally one-fifth of the tofu sticks and some cilantro leaves. Fold the left and right edges of the rice paper over the ends of the filling. Pull the lower edge upward and roll the package up from the bottom. Do exactly the same for the 4 other sheets and the remaining filling ingredients.

4 To make the dip, whisk together the peanut butter, soy sauce, oil, and agave syrup. Toast the sesame seeds in a dry pan, crush slightly using a mortar and pestle, and stir most of them into the dip. Garnish with the remaining sesame seeds and cilantro leaves. Pack up the rolls and dip separately to take with you.

For the rolls
5½oz (150g) tofu
1 heaped tbsp red Thai curry paste
1 tbsp orange juice
about 2 tbsp olive oil
sea salt
freshly ground black pepper
1¾oz (50g) green tea soba noodles
  (or regular soba noodles)
¼ cucumber
1 carrot
small bunch of cilantro
5 spring roll wrappers, each 8½in
  (22cm) in diameter

For the dip
2 level tbsp crunchy peanut butter
1 tbsp soy sauce
1½ tbsp sesame oil
1 tsp agave syrup
1 tsp sesame seeds
1 tsp cilantro leaves

TIP You can vary the vegetables as you like. Instead of cilantro, mint tastes very refreshing, particularly in the summer.

**Makes 2–3 snack portions
(8–10 rollmops)**
Preparation: 30 minutes
+ 2–3 days marinating time

EGGPLANT ROLLMOPS

You definitely won't find these in anyone else's lunch box! These unusual eggplant rolls are the ultimate proof that vegetable snacks are unbelievably versatile and exceptionally delicious. The spicy marinade gives the eggplant the most amazing flavor. Whether eaten with bread, straight from the jar, or as an embellishment for a salad or other dish, you can keep a container of these in your office for every eventuality.

For the marinade
¾ cup (175ml) white wine vinegar
3 tbsp golden granulated sugar
1 tbsp sea salt
6–8 juniper berries
black peppercorns (optional)
3–4 bay leaves

For the rollmops
2 eggplants
sea salt
1 onion
3 pickles
1 tbsp medium-strength mustard,
    such as Dijon
1 tsp sea salt
1 tsp freshly ground pepper

1 To make the marinade, bring 2 cups (500ml) water to a boil in a saucepan with the vinegar, sugar, salt, juniper, and peppercorns to taste (if using) and bay leaves, then remove from the heat and set aside.

2 For the rollmops, trim off the eggplant stalks. Cut lengthwise into ¼–½in (5mm–1cm) thick slices. Salt the slices on both sides. Lay them on a thick layer of paper towels and leave for 10 minutes, weighed down with a cutting board in order to remove the liquid.

3 Bring some generously salted water to a boil in a large saucepan and boil the eggplant pieces for 5 minutes over medium heat. Remove the slices from the water using a slotted spoon and leave to drain. Peel the onion and slice into thin strips. Likewise, cut the pickles into strips.

4 Spread the eggplant slices with mustard, season with 1 tsp more sea salt and the pepper, and top each piece with strips of pickle and onion. Roll them up and secure each using a toothpick. Layer the rollmops in a large jar. Cover with the warm marinade and leave to infuse for 2–3 days.

**Makes 2 snack portions
(8 cakes)**
Preparation: 30 minutes
+ 12 hours infusing time

BROCCOLI CAKES
WITH MANGO AND AVOCADO SALSA

1 To make the salsa, halve the tomatoes, remove the stalks and seeds, and chop finely. Peel the mango and avocado and remove the stones, then chop finely. Slice the chili lengthwise, remove the seeds, and slice into short, thin strips. Peel the onion and chop finely. Mix the prepared ingredients in a bowl with the cilantro. Add the lime juice, agave syrup, and salt to taste. Leave the salsa to infuse in the fridge for 12 hours.

2 For the cakes, wash the broccoli, and peel and chop the onion. Put in a food processor with the cilantro leaves, purée until smooth, then decant into a bowl.

3 Use a balloon whisk to combine the chickpea flour with the spices, salt, pepper, and linseed in a bowl. Add the dry mixture to the broccoli mixture and work everything together with your hands until you have a firm consistency. Divide the mix into 8 portions and shape each into a small, flat cake.

4 Heat the oil in a pan and fry the cakes on both sides over medium heat until golden brown. Package up the broccoli cakes and the salsa separately. These taste great either warm or cold.

For the salsa
2 tomatoes
½ small mango
½ small avocado
1 small red chile
1 small red onion
1 tbsp finely chopped cilantro
    leaves
1 tbsp lime juice
1 tsp agave syrup
½ tsp sea salt

For the cakes
1 cup (100g) chopped broccoli
1 small red onion
1 tbsp finely chopped cilantro
    leaves
3 tbsp chickpea flour
pinch of curry powder
pinch of ground cumin
pinch of ground ginger
pinch of chili powder
½ tsp sea salt
pinch of freshly ground black
    pepper
1 tbsp ground linseed
5 tbsp olive oil

TIP

People who aren't crazy about avocado can just make a pure mango salsa. Simply leave out the avocado and use double the quantity of mango.

Nougat rapidly softens at room temperature or in your hands, which is why you should shape the mixture with teaspoons and then just round it off with your hands.

¾ cup (85g) slivered almonds
5½oz (150g) firm vegan nougat
1oz (30g) hazelnut brittle
2¾oz (80g) vegan dark chocolate
½ tbsp coconut oil

SUPER CRUNCHY ALMOND NUT BALLS

1 Toast the almonds in a dry pan until golden brown. At the same time, heat the nougat in a heatproof bowl over a saucepan of simmering water. Finely crumble the toasted almonds into a small bowl and mix with the crumbled brittle. Work them into the nougat until evenly distributed and leave the mixture to chill for 20 minutes.

2 As soon as the nougat mixture is firm, but still malleable, form it into 10 balls. Let the balls chill once again for 20 minutes to firm up. Melt the dark chocolate with the oil in a heatproof bowl over a saucepan of simmering water. Use a fork to help you dip each ball into the chocolate, then set each on a cooling rack. Put into the fridge immediately and keep them there until ready to eat or pack up.

Makes 10
Preparation: 15 minutes
+ 1–2 hours chilling time

1½ tbsp (20g) coconut oil
½ cup (15g) crunchy vegan chocolate cereal
½ cup (100g) date paste (from a health food store)
½ cup (50g) ground hazelnuts
½ cup (50g) ground almonds
1oz (30g) shredded coconut

ENERGY BALLS WITH CHOCO POPS

1 Heat the oil in a small pan over low heat. Slightly crush the chocolate cereal and mix with the oil, date paste, hazelnuts, and almonds to create an even mixture that you can shape easily.

2 Spread the coconut on a plate. Shape 10 balls from the date and nut mixture and roll them in the coconut, pressing it in gently to make it stick. Chill the energy balls for 1–2 hours.

SOUPS & SALADS

creamy soups, stews & salads from all over the world

GAZPACHO

Southern Spain and Portugal encapsulated in soup form! This highly nutritious cold soup is traditionally prepared from uncooked vegetables and white bread. Tomato, onion, paprika, and cucumber combine beautifully, with ginger playing a role, too, in this less-traditional recipe. Gazpacho is perfect for hot summer days—transport it in an insulated container for a cooling and filling meal.

3 thick slices of white bread
7 ripe tomatoes, about 1lb 2oz
    (500g) in total
1 small onion
1 garlic clove (optional)
½in (1.5cm) piece of fresh ginger
1 red pepper
½ cucumber
1 cup (250ml) tomato juice
1 tbsp lime juice
2½ tbsp olive oil, plus extra
    if needed
1 tbsp red wine vinegar
1 tsp sweet smoked paprika
½ tsp sea salt
freshly ground black pepper
pinch of sugar
1 tbsp finely chopped basil leaves

1 Remove the crusts from the white bread and cut into rough cubes. Soak in lukewarm water. Cut an x in the base of each tomato, place in a bowl, pour boiling water over it, then blanch in iced water to cool them down. The skins should just peel off. Peel, quarter, and remove the core and seeds. Peel and finely chop the onion, garlic (if using), and ginger.

2 Cut the pepper in half lengthwise and remove the core and seeds. Peel the cucumber, cut in half lengthwise, and remove the core. Chop about one-quarter of the pepper and cucumber into very small cubes and set aside. Chop the rest roughly.

3 Squeeze out the bread cubes thoroughly. Put them in a food processor with the tomatoes, onion, garlic, ginger, roughly chopped vegetables, tomato juice, lime juice, oil, and vinegar and purée well. Season to taste with paprika, salt, pepper, and sugar. Add as much oil or water as you need to make the soup the desired consistency. Chill for around 2 hours (or overnight). Pack up the soup and finely chopped vegetables separately and scatter the vegetables and basil over the soup just before serving. Or simply stir everything together before transporting.

Makes 2 large or 4 small
portions
Preparation: 30 minutes
+ 20 minutes cooking time

SQUASH SOUP
WITH CARAMELIZED GINGER

1 Peel the potatoes, onion, garlic, and about one-third of the ginger
and coarsely chop them all into cubes. Halve the squash and
remove the soft center and seeds. Coarsely chop the squash,
including the skin. Heat the oil in a pan and sauté all the chopped
ingredients over medium heat. Pour over the stock and cook
everything for about 10 minutes, until soft.

2 Purée the vegetable chunks in the soup using a handheld
blender. Stir in the coconut milk, salt, pepper, nutmeg, and
cinnamon and simmer everything for a further 5–10 minutes
over low heat.

3 Meanwhile, carefully melt the sugar in a heavy-based pan over
medium heat, without stirring. Peel the remaining ginger, slice it
into julienne strips, and lightly caramelize these in the sugar. Remove
from the pan and leave to cool.

4 Leave the soup to cool and then chill. Pack up the soup, ginger
strips, sour cream, and parsley separately. To serve, briefly warm
the soup, stir in a spoonful of sour cream, and then sprinkle some
parsley and strips of ginger over it.

2 potatoes
1 onion
1 garlic clove
1¼in (3cm) piece of fresh ginger
1 small Hokkaido squash, about
    1lb 2oz (500g) in total
oil, for frying
2½ cups (600ml) hot vegetable stock
½ cup (100ml) coconut milk
½ tsp sea salt
pinch of freshly ground black
    pepper
pinch of freshly ground nutmeg
pinch of ground cinnamon
¼ cup (40g) brown sugar
2 tsp vegan sour cream
3 tbsp roughly chopped flat-leaf
    parsley leaves

TIP

If you don't have any way of heating the soup
at work, you can heat it at home and bring it
along in a vacuum flask to keep it warm.

1lb 2oz (500g) broccoli
1 small onion
1 tbsp canola oil
½ tbsp vegan margarine
1 tbsp all-purpose flour
1½ tbsp white wine
2 cups (500ml) vegetable stock
½ cup (100g) oat cream, or other
   plant-based cream
½ tsp sea salt
pinch of freshly ground white
   pepper
pinch of freshly ground nutmeg
2 tsp slivered almonds

BROCCOLI CREAM SOUP

1 Remove the broccoli stalk, split it into florets, and cut these into equal-sized pieces. Peel and finely chop the onion. Heat the oil in a large, high-sided pan, and sauté the onion over medium heat. Add the margarine and broccoli, dust with the flour, and sauté for around 2 minutes until the flour has combined with the other ingredients (it must not brown). Deglaze the pan with the wine and gradually pour in the stock, stirring continuously. Pour in the cream and cook for 5–10 minutes until the broccoli is soft. Purée with a handheld blender and season the soup to taste with salt, pepper, and nutmeg.

2 Toast the slivered almonds in a dry pan. To serve, briefly heat the soup and then scatter over the almonds, or just stir these into the soup before transporting.

6 carrots, about 1lb 2oz (500g)
   in total
½ medium parsnip
½ medium sweet potato
½in (1.5cm) piece of fresh ginger
2 cups (500ml) vegetable stock
½ tsp sea salt
pinch of freshly ground white
   pepper
pinch of ground coriander
pinch of freshly ground nutmeg
2 tsp sesame seeds
4 tbsp (50g) vegan sour cream

CREAMED CARROT SOUP

1 Peel the carrots and slice thinly, then peel the parsnip and sweet potato and chop into roughly ½in (1cm) cubes. Peel the ginger and chop finely. Bring the stock to a boil in a saucepan, add the carrots, parsnip, sweet potato, and ginger, cover, and cook over low heat for around 20 minutes until soft.

2 If desired, take a few carrot slices out of the pan and set aside. Use a handheld blender to purée the remaining vegetables in the stock. Then return the reserved carrot slices to the pan. Season the soup to taste with salt, pepper, coriander, and nutmeg, leave to cool, then chill.

3 Toast the sesame seeds in a dry pan. If you wish, you can stir the sesame seeds into the soup before transporting. Pack up the sour cream separately to take with you. To serve, briefly heat the soup, then sprinkle over the sesame seeds (unless you have already added them), and add a spoonful of sour cream.

Makes 2 large portions
Preparation: 10 minutes
+ 40 minutes cooking time

GRANDMA'S PEARL BARLEY STEW

Everyone knows that grandma makes the best stew. But where grandma used bacon back in the day, here we have a vegetable version that uses delicate cubes of smoked tofu. This is a warming, filling soupy bowlful, with little round grains of pearl barley and hearty root vegetables. Just perfect on a cold day: bolstering and warming, like a hug in a bowl.

2 carrots
1 small piece of celeriac
10oz (300g) waxy potatoes
1 leek
2 tbsp oil
½ cup (100g) pearl barley
4¼ cups (1 liter) vegetable stock
2–3 sprigs of lovage, or parsley or celery leaves, if you can't find lovage
7oz (200g) smoked tofu
sea salt
freshly ground black pepper

1 Peel the carrots, halve lengthwise, and then slice. Peel the celeriac and potatoes and chop into bite-size cubes. Wash the leek well and remove the root and the outer leaves. Slice into rings.

2 Heat 1 tbsp of the oil in a pan and sauté the carrots, celeriac, potatoes, and leek. Add the pearl barley and continue to sauté for a short time. Pour over the vegetable stock and add the lovage. Cook everything over medium heat for 40 minutes. Stir every so often and make sure there is enough liquid, adding water if necessary.

3 In the meantime, chop the tofu into rough cubes. Heat the remaining 1 tbsp of oil in a pan and sauté the tofu over medium heat until golden brown on all sides.

4 Remove the lovage from the stew and stir in the tofu. Season to taste. Leave to cool, then chill. Reheat briefly before serving.

SPICY QUINOA CHILI

Protein-rich quinoa is a truly versatile ingredient. Here it takes the leading role in a spicy chili, with supporting parts being played by pepper, tomatoes, sweetcorn, kidney beans, and spices. Chili is an obvious choice for lunch: it is the perfect dish to prepare a day in advance, because it usually tastes even better once the flavors have infused for a day or so.

1 Run the quinoa under water in a strainer until the water flows clear, then cook it in the simmering stock for about 15 minutes, or according to the package instructions. Drain in a strainer, rinse with cold water, and set aside. Slice the pepper and chile in half lengthwise, and remove the seeds. Chop the pepper into bite-sized cubes and finely chop the chile. Peel the onion and garlic and chop finely.

2 Heat the oil in a large pan and sauté the pepper, chile, onion, and garlic over medium heat. Add the tomato purée and briefly sauté this with the other ingredients. Add the tomatoes and simmer everything for 5 minutes.

3 Drain the sweetcorn and beans in a strainer, rinse with cold water, and fold into the sauce with the quinoa. Let everything continue to simmer for 5 minutes. Adjust the flavor by adding lime juice, salt, pepper, chili powder, oregano, cumin, and maple syrup to taste. Leave to cool, chill, and briefly reheat before serving.

½ cup (100g) quinoa
1 cup (250ml) vegetable stock
½ green pepper
1 red chile
1 small onion
1 garlic clove
1½ tbsp olive oil
2½ tbsp tomato purée
14oz (400g) can of chopped tomatoes
1 cup (140g) sweetcorn
7oz (200g) kidney beans
1 tbsp lime juice
pinch of sea salt
pinch of freshly ground white
   pepper
1 tsp chili powder, or to taste
pinch of dried oregano
pinch of ground cumin
1 tsp maple syrup

TIP

A baguette goes really well with this, or try a baked sweet potato. To prepare the potato, preheat the oven to 350°F (180°C), scrub the sweet potato, pat it dry, place it on a baking sheet, and sprinkle with 1 tbsp sea salt. Bake in the center of the oven for 40–45 minutes. To serve, slice into the sweet potato, press the halves apart but do not separate, then fill with the quinoa chili.

Each dresses 1 portion of salad
Preparation: 10 minutes each
+ infusing time

DRESSINGS AND DIPS

These create endless options for your lunches. With just a little experimentation, you can pair up each of the dressings below in new ways with a huge variety of seasonal salads. Creamy dips such as Vegan Mayonnaise and Tartar Sauce (see right) are the perfect finishing touch for potatoes, roast vegetables, burgers, wraps, or falafel.

1 small shallot
3 tbsp vinegar (white wine, red
   wine, or herb vinegar)
½ tsp sea salt
pinch of freshly ground white pepper
pinch of sugar
touch of Dijon mustard
½ cup extra virgin oil (such as
   sunflower, safflower, or olive oil)

VINAIGRETTE

Peel and finely chop the shallot. Stir together with the vinegar, salt, pepper, sugar, and mustard in a bowl. Gradually add the oil, stirring continuously, and mix until everything is emulsified.

 TIP For the vinaigrette, the ratio of vinegar to oil should be 1:3, so the dressing isn't too acidic.

½ cup (150g) vegan sour cream
1 tbsp Dijon mustard
½ bunch of flat leaf parsley
1 tsp linseed oil
1 tbsp olive oil
pinch of sea salt
pinch of freshly ground black pepper
1 tsp agave syrup, or to taste

SOUR CREAM AND PARSLEY DRESSING

Mix the sour cream with the mustard in a bowl. Pick the leaves from the parsley stalks, chop them finely, and fold into the cream mixture. Gradually stir in the linseed and olive oils. Season the dressing to taste with salt, pepper, and agave syrup.

½ bunch of chives
1 cup (250g) soy yogurt, or other
   plant-based yogurt
juice of ½ lemon
1 tbsp walnut oil
sea salt
freshly ground black pepper
pinch of sugar, or to taste

SPEEDY YOGURT AND WALNUT DRESSING

Snip the chives finely. Stir the soy yogurt, lemon juice, and oil together with a whisk until smooth, then fold in the chives. Season the dressing to taste with salt, pepper, and sugar.

VEGAN MAYONNAISE

Process the soy milk with ½ cup (100ml) oil in a food processor until smooth. Add the vinegar, salt, and mustard and process everything again. Slowly trickle in the remaining oil with the processor running. Then add the potatoes, until you have a creamy consistency. Season to taste with pepper, sugar, curry powder (if using), and lemon juice (if using). Store in the fridge until ready to use.

TIP The mayonnaise will keep in the fridge for 7–10 days. It tastes great with Little Potato Cakes (see p25) or Spicy Kale Chips (see p29) and is the perfect finishing touch for sandwiches and burgers (see page 94–102).

- 1 cup (250ml) soy milk, or other plant-based milk
- ¾ cup (200ml) extra virgin olive oil
- 2 tbsp white wine vinegar
- 1 tsp sea salt
- 1 tbsp medium-strength mustard
- ½ cup (100g) russet potatoes, cooked and mashed
- pinch of freshly ground white pepper
- pinch of sugar
- pinch of curry powder (optional)
- 1 tsp lemon juice (optional)

TARTAR SAUCE

Stir together the mayonnaise, cucumber relish, capers, chervil, and tarragon in a small bowl until well combined. Snip the chives finely and fold into the tartar sauce. Season to taste and chill.

TIP The tartar sauce can be tweaked by adding finely chopped onion. It tastes really great with Spicy Oven-Roasted Cauliflower (see p26), with wraps (see pp108–13), or with Little Quinoa Balls (see p132).

- 1 × recipe Vegan Mayonnaise (see above)
- 2 tbsp cucumber relish (from a jar)
- 1 tsp capers, rinsed and finely chopped
- pinch of dried chervil
- pinch of dried tarragon
- ½ bunch of chives
- sea salt
- freshly ground black pepper

THOUSAND ISLAND DRESSING

Seed and very finely chop the pepper and chile. Finely chop the cucumber. Pick the leaves from the parsley stalks, then chop them finely. Stir together the mayonnaise, yogurt, ketchup, and cream in a bowl. Add the sambal oelek, lime juice, salt, and pepper to taste. Fold the pepper, chile, cucumber, and parsley into the mayonnaise mixture. Leave the dressing to infuse for 30 minutes, then adjust the seasonings if you want. Chill until ready to use.

- ¼ green pepper
- ¼ red chile
- 1 cucumber
- ½ bunch of flat leaf parsley
- ½ cup (100g) Vegan Mayonnaise (see above)
- ½ cup (150g) plant-based yogurt
- 3 tbsp tomato ketchup
- 2 tbsp oat cream
- 4 drops of sambal oelek, or to taste
- 2 tsp lime juice, or to taste
- ½ tsp sea salt
- ½ tsp freshly ground white pepper

VEGAN MAYONNAISE

**SOUR CREAM
AND PARSLEY
DRESSING**

**THOUSAND
ISLAND
DRESSING**

TARTAR SAUCE

VINAIGRETTE

SPEEDY YOGURT AND
WALNUT DRESSING

Makes 1 large or 2 small portions
Preparation: 20 minutes
+ 12 hours marinating time

GREEK FARMER'S SALAD

1 For the "feta," peel the onion and garlic (if using) and chop them finely. Add them to a bowl and combine with the lemon juice, oil, vinegar, salt, pepper, herbes de Provençe, and chili powder to create a marinade. Slice the tofu into ½in (1cm) cubes and put it in a freezer bag with the marinade. Press the air out of the bag and seal it tightly shut. Marinate the tofu in the fridge for 12 hours.

2 For the salad, peel the cucumber, slice it in half, remove the seeds, and cut into bite-sized pieces. Similarly chop the tomato into bite-sized pieces, removing the core in the process. Peel and halve the onion and slice it into thin rings, or chop it finely. Halve the peppers, remove the seeds, then chop into bite-sized strips. Roughly chop the oregano. Add all the prepared salad ingredients to a bowl with the olives.

3 Stir together the lemon juice, agave syrup, oil, vinegar, salt, and pepper to create a delicious vinaigrette and use it to dress the salad. Scatter over the "feta" cubes. This tastes great with some fresh flatbread, ideally warmed, on the side.

TIP You can use the "feta" marinade oil again by adding more herbs and spices to freshen it up once more before marinating another batch of tofu.

For the "feta"
1 small red onion
1 garlic clove (optional)
squeeze of lemon juice
½ cup (100ml) extra virgin olive oil
1 tbsp herb vinegar
1 tsp sea salt
1 tsp ground mixed colored peppercorns
1 tbsp herbes de Provençe
pinch of chili powder
9oz (250g) smoked tofu

For the salad
½ cucumber
1 large beef tomato
1 red onion
2 small yellow peppers
2 tbsp oregano leaves
1¾oz (50g) black olives, pits removed
1 tsp lemon juice
½ tsp agave syrup
1 tsp extra virgin olive oil
1 tsp white wine vinegar
½ tsp sea salt
pinch of freshly ground black pepper

PANZANELLA—
ITALIAN BREAD SALAD

This tastes like a little piece of Italy. A traditional salad, it is really filling thanks to the bread pieces, which are coated with good-quality olive oil before being baked. Cucumber and cherry tomatoes bring a wonderful freshness. Simple and good, the only thing missing from this lunchbox is a view of Italy!

5 slices of french baguette
8 tbsp extra virgin olive oil
½ small cucumber
5 cherry tomatoes
2 green onions
3–4 sprigs of basil
2 tbsp balsamic vinegar
squeeze of lemon juice
sea salt
freshly ground black pepper

1 Preheat the oven to as high as it will go. Cut the baguette slices into bite-sized cubes and put them in a bowl. Add 4 tbsp of the oil and mix together well with your hands.

2 Line a baking sheet with parchment paper and spread the bread out over it. Bake in the center of the oven for about 10 minutes, until crisp (keep an eye on it, as you don't want it to burn). Remove from the oven and allow to cool.

3 Meanwhile, chop the cucumber into bite-sized chunks. Halve the tomatoes. Trim the green onions, then slice into rings. Pick off and shred the basil leaves. Mix together the cucumber, tomatoes, green onions, basil, and cubes of bread.

4 Stir together the remaining oil with the vinegar, lemon juice, salt, and pepper to make the dressing. Transport the dressing and salad separately and ideally combine them 20 minutes before you are ready to eat, so the bread can absorb the dressing.

Makes 1 large or 2 small portions
Preparation: 25 minutes

ANDALUCIAN ASPARAGUS SALAD

Two varieties of regal asparagus spears are found in this Andalucian salad: an unusual combination with zesty oranges, sweet dates, and delicately bitter olives. This is a fruity and piquant spring salad, which makes for a tasty, interesting, and aesthetically pleasing lunch.

1 Chop the seitan into ½in (1cm) pieces. Remove the woody ends from all the asparagus spears. Peel the lower one-third of the stem of each green asparagus spear. Slice all the asparagus spears diagonally to make 1½in (4cm) long pieces. Set the asparagus tips aside.

2 Finely chop the dates. Finely grate 1 orange, or use a zester to make fine strips. Cut both oranges in half and squeeze the juice into a bowl.

3 Heat the oil in a pan and sauté the seitan and the asparagus pieces (not the tips) for a short time over medium heat. Stir in the olives and orange zest. Add the vinegar, soy sauce, and orange juice. Mix in both types of paprika, as well as the salt, pepper, allspice, and lime juice. Let cook over low heat for 5 minutes. Finally, fold in the asparagus tips and dates and cook briefly. The salad tastes great warm or cold.

3½oz (100g) seitan
15 green asparagus spears
15 white asparagus spears
5 pitted dates
2 small unwaxed oranges
2 tbsp extra virgin olive oil
1¾oz (50g) pitted black olives
1 tbsp balsamic vinegar
1 tbsp soy sauce
½ tsp hot paprika
1 tsp sweet smoked paprika
½ tsp sea salt
pinch of freshly ground black pepper
pinch of ground allspice
1 tbsp lime juice

ZUCCHINI "SPAGHETTI" SALAD
WITH WILD GARLIC PESTO

Vegetable noodles are a fantastic way of enjoying gluten-free spaghetti. This spaghetti salad is served with homemade wild garlic pesto and doesn't even need to be cooked, which makes it super-simple and really practical, especially when you find yourself short on time.

For the salad
2 medium zucchini
1⅓ cup (200g) cherry tomatoes

For the pesto
⅓ cup (50g) pine nuts
2oz (60g) wild garlic
5 tbsp extra virgin olive oil
2 tsp yeast flakes
½ tsp lemon juice
1 tsp sea salt
pinch of freshly ground black pepper
pinch of sugar

1 To make the salad, use a spiralizer to cut the zucchini into long, thin "spaghetti" shapes. Alternatively, use a potato peeler to make long, thin slices and then cut these up into fine strips with a knife. Put the zucchini "spaghetti" into a bowl. Halve the tomatoes and mix them in with the zucchini.

2 To make the wild garlic pesto, lightly toast the pine nuts in a dry pan until they begin to release their aroma. Add the wild garlic, oil, yeast flakes, lemon juice, salt, pepper, and sugar. Purée the ingredients to your desired consistency (fine or coarse) using a handheld blender.

3 Either mix together the pesto and zucchini spaghetti salad before transporting, or pack them up separately to take with you. Serve the salad cold.

Makes 1 large or 2 small
portions
Preparation: 20 minutes

FENNEL, BANANA, AND FUSILLI SALAD
WITH ORANGE YOGURT DRESSING

Boring meals are history! In this delicious fennel and banana salad, flamboyant flavors come together to create a genuine taste sensation. Distinctive fennel really comes into its own here, while banana, apple, pasta, and a slightly sweet dressing prove the ideal partners.

1 To make the salad, cook the fusilli according to the package instructions (usually 8–10 minutes) in salted water. Meanwhile, remove the tough core from the fennel, cut off the stalks, then finely grate the bulb. Peel and slice the banana. Peel the apple, remove the core, and grate it finely. Drain the pasta in a colander and plunge into cold water to stop the cooking, then drain again. Fold in the fennel, banana, and apple.

2 For the dressing, mix together the yogurt, orange juice, oil, vinegar, curry powder, salt, and pepper in a small bowl. Toast the pine nuts in a dry pan until golden brown, then let cool. Pick the leaves from the parsley stalks and chop them finely. Fold the dressing, pine nuts, and parsley into the pasta mixture. Add lemon juice to taste and a little more salt and pepper, if you like.

For the salad
1 cup (100g) fusilli pasta
sea salt
1 fennel bulb
1 large banana
½ apple

For the dressing
¾ cup (200g) soy yogurt, or other plant-based yogurt
6 tbsp orange juice
2 tbsp extra virgin olive oil
3 tbsp orange vinegar, or white wine or herb vinegar
½–1 heaped tbsp mild curry powder
1½ tsp sea salt
½ tsp freshly ground black pepper
⅓ cup (50g) pine nuts
small bunch of parsley
squeeze of lemon juice

Makes 1 portion
Preparation: 25 minutes

KALE, QUINOA, AND SWEETCORN SALAD

Kale is a kind of winter cabbage. This healthy vegetable is super-fashionable and, like all other varieties of cabbage, is high in vitamin C. Here it is served in a winning combination with quinoa, sweetcorn, and almonds. This is a superfood salad that is in a class of its own.

⅓ cup (50g) quinoa
½ cup (100ml) vegetable stock
1 onion
4 tbsp extra virgin olive oil
3 cups (200g) chopped kale
1–2 green onions, green parts only
2 tbsp (20g) blanched almonds
2 tsp sesame seeds
½ cup (100g) frozen sweetcorn
3 tbsp lemon juice
1 tsp herb or white wine vinegar
3 tbsp sesame oil
1 tbsp agave syrup
sea salt
freshly ground black pepper

1 Rinse the quinoa in a strainer until the water runs clear, then simmer in the stock according to the package instructions (usually about 15 minutes). Peel and finely chop the onion.

2 Heat 1 tbsp of the olive oil in a sauté pan and sauté the onion over high heat for 1 minute. Add the kale and continue to sauté for 5 minutes. Pour off any liquid, set the pan aside, and let cool.

3 Drain the cooked quinoa into a strainer, rinse with cold water, and allow to drain. Slice the green onions into rings. Roughly chop the almonds. Toast the sesame seeds in a dry pan until golden brown. Drain the sweetcorn in a strainer. Mix together the lemon juice, vinegar, sesame oil, remaining 3 tbsp of olive oil, and agave syrup in a bowl to make the dressing and season to taste with salt and pepper.

4 Combine the kale and onion mixture with the quinoa, green onions, almonds, sesame seeds, and sweetcorn in a bowl. Stir in the dressing and adjust the seasoning once again.

MACARONI "CHEESE" SALAD

Why not use this ever-popular comfort food dish as the inspiration for conjuring up a cold salad? It doesn't need any "cheese"—the cashews and mustard help create a vegan version that is a total winner.

1 Cook the macaroni in salted water according to the package instructions, until al dente. Drain in a colander, refresh under running cold water, then allow to drain. Set aside.

2 To make the sauce, peel the sweet potato and carrot and chop into ¾in (2cm) cubes. Peel and quarter the onion. Boil the sweet potato, carrot, and onion in the stock until tender (about 10 minutes). Drain and reserve about 1 cup (250ml) of the stock. Peel the garlic (if using) and use a food processor to purée the garlic, sweet potato, carrots, and onion with the reserved stock, cashews, mustard, salt, lemon juice, pepper, paprika, and margarine until smooth.

3 Halve the tomatoes. Trim the scallions and chop them finely. Drain or defrost the peas and sweetcorn and pat them dry with paper towels. Mix together the macaroni, sauce, tomatoes, scallions, peas, and sweetcorn.

For the macaroni
2½ cups (250g) macaroni
sea salt
4 cherry tomatoes
½ bunch of scallions
⅓ cup (50g) frozen peas
⅓ cup (50g) frozen sweetcorn

For the sauce
1 small sweet potato
1 small carrot
1 small onion
1¾ cups (375ml) vegetable stock
1 small garlic clove (optional)
1oz (30g) cashew nuts
½ tsp Dijon mustard
½ tsp sea salt
squeeze of lemon juice
pinch of freshly ground black
 pepper
½ tsp sweet smoked paprika
1½ tbsp vegan margarine

TIP

The sauce is also excellent
for topping grilled dishes,
or used as a dip.

Makes 2 large portions
Preparation: 30 minutes

ASIAN NOODLE SALAD

Do you ever feel like indulging in a bit of overseas travel on your lunch break? The mie noodles, bok choy, and bean sprouts in this Asian salad will whisk you right off to Asia! This is a fresh, healthy, and completely vegan alternative to ordering take-out.

For the salad
9oz (250g) vegan mie noodles
   (from an Asian store)
sea salt
½ red pepper
½ onion
2¾oz (75g) bean sprouts
1 tbsp canola oil
1½ cups (100g) chopped bok choy
1 tbsp sesame seeds
2 sprigs of cilantro

For the dip
1 tbsp peanut butter
½ tbsp rice vinegar
½ tsp lime juice
1 tsp agave syrup
pinch of ground cilantro
½ tsp sea salt
pinch of freshly ground white
   pepper

1 To make the salad, cook the noodles in lightly salted water according to the package instructions. Drain in a colander, refresh under running cold water, allow to drain thoroughly, then set aside in a large bowl. Remove the seeds from the pepper, and slice into strips. Peel the onion and slice thinly. Put the bean sprouts into a strainer and rinse under cold water, then let drain.

2 Heat the oil in a wok and sauté the bok choy, pepper, and onion over medium heat. Add the bean sprouts and sauté them briefly, too—the vegetables should remain nice and crunchy. Add the vegetables to the noodles in the bowl. Toast the sesame seeds in a dry pan until golden brown. Pick the leaves from the cilantro sprigs and chop them finely. Add the sesame seeds and cilantro to the salad ingredients.

3 To make the dip, put the peanut butter into a small bowl along with the vinegar, lime juice, and agave syrup and stir until smooth. Add the ground cilantro, salt, and pepper to taste. Pack up the salad and the dip separately to take with you. To serve, add the dip to the salad and mix all the ingredients carefully.

MEXICAN PEPPER SALAD

1 To make the salad, quarter the peppers, remove the seeds, then chop into bite-sized pieces. Quarter the tomatoes, remove the core and seeds, then chop into small cubes. Peel and finely chop the onion. Snip the chives finely. Drain the sweetcorn and beans in a colander, rinse under cold water, and allow to drain. Carefully mix all the prepared ingredients together in a bowl.

2 For the dressing, combine all the ingredients in a little bowl with a whisk. Add the dressing to the salad and carefully mix together.

 TIP Tortilla chips and Guacamole go wonderfully with this (see p30).

Makes 2 portions
Preparation: 20 minutes

For the salad
3 peppers, ideally red, yellow, and green
2 beef tomatoes
1 onion
½ bunch of chives
1 cup (140g) frozen sweetcorn
½ cup (125g) canned kidney beans

For the dressing
finely grated zest and juice of ½ unwaxed lime
1 tbsp white wine vinegar
2 tbsp extra virgin olive oil
½ tsp sea salt
pinch of freshly ground black pepper
pinch of chili powder
pinch of sugar

TUSCAN BEAN SALAD

1 Drain the beans in a colander, then transfer to a bowl. Peel and finely chop the shallot. Heat 3 tbsp oil from the sun-dried tomatoes in a small saucepan and sauté the shallot until it is transparent. Add the tomato purée and continue to cook briefly. Fold the shallot mixture into the beans.

2 Slice the sun-dried tomatoes into thin strips. Fold into the beans with the parsley, mint, and capers. Adjust the flavor to taste by adding salt, pepper, oregano, basil, vinegar, and agave syrup. Let the salad infuse for 12 hours. If necessary, adjust the seasoning again.

Makes 1 portion
Preparation: 15 minutes
+ 12 hours infusing time

1 cup (240g) canned navy or white kidney beans
1 shallot
1 cup (60g) sun-dried tomatoes in oil
1½ tbsp tomato purée
3 tbsp chopped parsley leaves
1 tbsp chopped mint leaves
½ tbsp capers, rinsed
½ tsp sea salt
pinch of freshly ground white pepper
pinch of dried oregano
pinch of dried basil
1½ tbsp white wine vinegar
½ tsp agave syrup

INDIAN CHICKPEA AND POMEGRANATE SALAD

A brand-new way to use this wonderful, tart-sweet fruit, the pomegranate seeds are combined exquisitely with chickpeas and an Indian-style mint and yogurt dressing. This is a valuable addition to any vegan lunchbox!

For the salad
1 scallion
½ red pepper
½ onion
½in (1.5cm) piece of fresh ginger
½ pomegranate
2½ cups (400g) chickpeas
3 tbsp pine nuts

For the dressing
1 tbsp soy yogurt, or other plant-
    based yogurt
1 tbsp chopped mint leaves
½ tsp sea salt
pinch of freshly ground white
    pepper
pinch of ground cumin
½ tsp garam masala
pinch of sugar

1 To make the salad, trim the scallion and slice into fine rings. Remove the seeds from the pepper, then cut into thin strips. Peel and finely chop the onion and ginger. Remove the seeds from the pomegranate. Put the chickpeas into a colander and rinse with cold water before allowing to drain. Put all the prepared ingredients into a bowl.

2 For the dressing, mix together the yogurt, mint, salt, pepper, cumin, garam masala, and sugar. Add the dressing to the salad in the bowl and carefully mix together. Toast the pine nuts in a dry pan until golden brown. Pack up the salad and pine nuts separately to take with you, or just combine them ahead of time.

Makes 1 large or 2 small portions
Preparation: 20 minutes
+ 30 minutes infusing time

ARABIAN LENTIL SALAD

Lentils are one of the best sources of protein. In this salad they are also a guaranteed winner in terms of flavor, thanks to the accompanying Arab-style spices. Dates balance things out with some added sweetness, while harissa lends the dish a mildly spicy flavor—all the ingredients work in perfect harmony to create a real lunchtime treat.

1 To make the salad, put the lentils into a colander, rinse under cold water, and allow to drain. Peel the cucumber, slice it in half lengthwise, remove the seeds, then chop into cubes. Quarter the tomato, remove the core and seeds, then chop finely. Slice the celery thinly. Pick the leaves from the herb stalks and chop finely. Cut the dates into small pieces. Peel and finely chop the shallot and garlic. Heat the oil in a pan and sauté the shallot over medium heat, then add the garlic. Allow the mixture to cool, then mix with the prepared ingredients in a bowl.

2 To make the dressing, stir together the lime juice, oil, salt, pepper, cumin, allspice, agave syrup, and harissa. Add the dressing to the salad in the bowl. Leave to infuse for at least 30 minutes, then taste again and adjust the seasoning, if desired, with more salt and pepper.

For the salad
2 cups (400g) cooked green lentils
½ cucumber
1 very large tomato
2 celery sticks
¼ bunch of flat leaf parsley
¼ bunch of mint
5 pitted dates
1 shallot
1 small garlic clove
1 tbsp olive oil

For the dressing
juice of 1 small lime
1½ tbsp extra virgin olive oil
½ tsp sea salt
pinch of freshly ground black pepper
pinch of ground cumin
pinch of ground allspice
1 tsp agave syrup
½ tsp harissa

TIP

This salad is ideal for preparing in advance for your lunch because its flavor really improves when left to infuse.

ASIAN
CAULIFLOWER AND POTATO SALAD

7oz (200g) new potatoes
sea salt
½ small cauliflower
½ small eggplant
1 small garlic clove
1 red chile
1¾oz (50g) cashew nuts
2 sprigs of cilantro
1½ tbsp canola oil
½ cup (120ml) coconut milk
pinch of freshly ground black
    pepper
pinch of ground cumin
pinch of ground cinnamon
pinch of ground allspice

1 Scrub the potatoes and cook them with the skins on in salted water for 20–25 minutes. Drain, allow them to cool slightly, then peel and cut into thick slices.

2 Meanwhile, split the cauliflower into florets. Cut off the eggplant stalk and cut into cubes. Peel and finely chop the garlic. Slice the chile in half lengthwise, remove the seeds, then chop finely. Toast the cashews in a dry pan until golden brown, let cool, then chop roughly. Pick the leaves from the cilantro stalks and chop finely.

3 Heat the oil in a large high-sided pan and sauté the garlic over medium heat. Add the cauliflower, eggplant, and chile and continue to cook until the vegetables are al dente. Add the coconut milk and season with salt, pepper, cumin, cinnamon, and allspice. Fold in the potatoes and transfer the mixture to a bowl. Scatter cashews and cilantro over the salad and let cool completely.

SANDWICHES, WRAPS, & ROLLS

from sandwiches to burgers—
spreads, toppings, & wraps

Makes 1 large or 2 small portions
Preparation: 10 minutes
+ 15 minutes cooking time

6 slices of whole-wheat bread
2½ tbsp homemade Ajvar
   (see below)
2½ tbsp vegan margarine

COLORFUL LITTLE TOAST SPIRALS

Transform even inferior sliced bread into an ingenious snack. These colorful little rolls with their Serbian vegetable relish are the perfect solution if you find yourself getting hungry between meals. Add a couple of vegetable sticks and just use the remaining Ajvar as a dip.

Preheat the oven to 400°F (200°C). Remove the crusts from the slices of bread and roll them flat with a rolling pin. Spread the Ajvar on top and roll them up. Melt the margarine in a pan and brush it over the toast rolls. Lay them next to each other in a casserole dish and bake in the center of the preheated oven for 15 minutes. These go wonderfully with a salad, vegetable sticks, or antipasti.

Makes about 9oz (250g)
Preparation: 10 minutes
+ 25 minutes cooking time
+ 20 minutes cooling time

3 large red peppers
½ large red chile
½ eggplant (halved lengthwise)
1 tbsp sunflower oil
1 tsp cider vinegar
pinch of sea salt
pinch of freshly ground white
   pepper
pinch of hot paprika
½ tsp agave syrup

QUICK AJVAR

1 Preheat the oven to 425°F (220°C). Line a baking sheet with parchment paper. Slice the peppers and chile in half lengthwise and remove the seeds. Remove the stalk from the eggplant. Lay the peppers, chile, and eggplant skin side up on the baking sheet. Bake in the center of the oven for about 25 minutes, until the skins have turned dark and are blistering. Remove the baking sheet from the oven and cover the vegetables with a clean, damp paper towel. Let cool for around 20 minutes.

2 Peel the peppers, chile, and eggplant and chop into large pieces. Put these into a food processor with the oil, vinegar, salt, pepper, paprika, and agave syrup and purée until creamy. Pour into a screw-top jar and store in the fridge.

TIP
To preserve your ajvar, put the sealed jar in an heatproof dish. Half-fill a large roasting pan with boiling water and place the dish in it. Cook for 25 minutes in an oven preheated to 400°F (200°C). Allow it to cool in the oven. It should keep for 3—4 months.

SPICY
TOMATO TARTARE
ON CRUNCHY CIABATTA

This can be packed up really quickly—toasted ciabatta in the box, delicious homemade tomato tartare with black olives in a container, and your snack is complete. Just unpack, assemble, and enjoy the crunchy bread and aromatic tartare sauce that melts in your mouth. So simple!

1 If desired, skin the tomatoes: to do this, score a cross into the skins on the opposite side from the stalks, place in a bowl, pour over boiling water, and leave briefly. Plunge into cold water so they don't start to cook; the skins should just peel off. Quarter them, remove the seeds, and finely chop the flesh. Finely chop the olives.

2 Mix the tomatoes and olives with the salt, pepper, lemon zest, 1 tsp of the lemon juice, 1 tbsp of the oil, vinegar, agave syrup, and basil. Taste and add extra lemon juice and possibly more salt and pepper, if you like.

3 Heat the remaining 1½ tbsp of oil in a large pan and toast the ciabatta slices in it on both sides until golden brown. Remove from the pan and let cool. Pack up the ciabatta and tomato tartare separately to take with you. To serve, simply spread the tomato tartare on the slices of bread.

4 ripe tomatoes
1¼oz (40g) pitted black olives
½ tsp sea salt
pinch of freshly ground mixed colored peppercorns
finely grated zest and juice of ½ unwaxed lemon
2½ tbsp extra virgin olive oil
½ tsp balsamic vinegar
½ tsp agave syrup
1–2 tbsp chopped basil leaves
4 slices of ciabatta bread

Each makes 1 jar
Preparation: 10 minutes
+ cooking time + draining and
infusing time

7oz (200g) smoked tofu (ideally
    strongly smoked)
1 cup (240g) canned kidney beans
½ tsp English, or spicy, mustard
pinch of ground ginger
1 large onion
3–4 tbsp olive oil
2 tsp dried marjoram
1 tsp chopped parsley leaves
sea salt
freshly ground black pepper

SMOKY PÂTÉ

1 Crumble the smoked tofu into little pieces and put it into a food
processor. Pour the kidney beans into a colander, let them drain
thoroughly, then add these to the food processor along with the
mustard and ginger.

2 Peel and finely chop the onion. Heat the oil in a pan and sauté the
onion over medium heat. Add to the food processor and purée
well to a creamy consistency. Fold in the marjoram and parsley and
season to taste with salt and pepper.

2 cups (500g) soy yogurt
2 tbsp vegan sour cream
2 tbsp good-quality pumpkin
    seed oil
1 tsp sea salt
pinch of freshly ground black
    pepper
3 tbsp pumpkin seeds

SOY LABNEH AND PUMPKIN SEED SPREAD

1 Put the yogurt into a strainer lined with a cheesecloth. Place this
over a bowl and leave in the fridge for 12 hours to drip. Squeeze
it and put the resulting soy labneh into a bowl. Purée it with the sour
cream, oil, salt, and pepper using a handheld blender.

2 Set aside a few pumpkin seeds for decorating, then finely chop
the remainder and toast them in a dry pan. Allow to cool slightly,
then fold them into the labneh. Pour into a well-sealed container and
sprinkle with the remaining pumpkin seeds.

SPICY "CREAM CHEESE" WITH PICKLES

1 Put the yogurt into a strainer lined with a cheesecloth. Place this over a bowl and leave in the fridge for 12 hours to drip. Squeeze it and put the resulting soy cheese into a bowl. Add the sour cream, margarine, both types of paprika, garlic powder, salt, pepper, tomato purée, and capers. Use a handheld blender to purée everything in the bowl until smooth.

2 Finely chop the pickles. Remove the seeds from the pepper. Peel the onion, then finely chop both this and the peppers. Fold the chopped ingredients into the cream cheese. Add chili powder to taste and let infuse for 4–5 hours.

2 cups (500g) soy yogurt
7 tbsp (80g) vegan sour cream
5 tbsp (70g) soft vegan margarine
2 tbsp mild paprika
¼ tbsp hot paprika
½ tsp garlic powder
1 tsp sea salt
1 tsp freshly ground white pepper
1 tsp tomato purée
2 tbsp (15g) capers, rinsed
2 pickles
½ small red pepper
1 small onion
pinch of chili powder

SANDWICH SPREAD

Bring the stock to a boil in a small saucepan. Peel and finely chop the onion and put in a bowl. Crumble in the rice cakes and mix in the hot stock, oil, tomato purée, chives, salt, pepper, marjoram, and sweet smoked paprika.

½ cup (125ml) vegetable stock
1 onion
14 rice cakes
1 tbsp sunflower oil
2½ tbsp tomato purée
2 tbsp chopped chives
½ tsp sea salt
pinch of freshly ground black pepper
½ tsp dried marjoram
pinch of sweet smoked paprika

SPICY RED LENTIL SPREAD

Rinse the lentils in a strainer and allow to drain thoroughly. Bring to a boil with the stock in small saucepan, cover, and cook for 15 minutes, then allow to cool. Mix the lentils and any remaining stock with the spices, salt, oil, and liquid smoke (if using), then purée until really smooth using a handheld blender.

TIP To go with all these spreads, just pack up your choice of fresh bread, Little Potato Cakes (see p25), or Zucchini Cake (see p121).

¼ cup (50g) red lentils
¾ cup (150ml) vegetable stock
½ tsp ground turmeric
½ tsp curry powder
½ tsp ground coriander
pinch of red pepper flakes
½ tsp sea salt
½ tbsp olive oil
2 drops of liquid smoke (optional; from a delicatessen or online)

HOT "CREAM CHEESE" SPRING SANDWICH

Bring a touch of spring to your lunchbox with radishes, cress, cucumber, and a delicious hot cashew "cream cheese." Quick and easy to prepare, this is a nondairy spread that works really well. Of course, it tastes great at other times of year, too.

For the hot cashew "cream cheese"
7oz (200g) cashew nuts
2 tsp lemon juice
2 tbsp olive oil
2 red chiles
2 tbsp yeast flakes
1 tsp sea salt
pinch of freshly ground black pepper
½ tsp sweet smoked paprika
5 drops of chili sauce (optional)

For the sandwiches
¼ cucumber
½ bunch of radishes
1 small bunch of cress
handful of salad leaves
4 slices of whole-wheat bread

1 To make the hot cashew "cream cheese," soak the cashews in cold water for 12 hours. Drain in a strainer, then purée thoroughly in a food processor with ½ cup (100ml) water, the lemon juice, and oil. Transfer to a bowl. Halve the chiles lengthwise, remove the seeds, and chop finely. Stir into the cashew mixture with the yeast flakes, salt, pepper, paprika, and chili sauce (if using) until well combined.

2 To make the sandwiches, peel the cucumber and slice it and the radishes thinly. Snip the cress with some scissors. Shred the salad leaves into little pieces.

3 Toast the slices of bread and spread the "cream cheese" mixture on them. Distribute the salad leaves between 2 slices of toast, top with the sliced cucumber and radishes, and sprinkle with the cress. Place the remaining slices of toast on top. If you like, split the toasts in half, then pack them into a well-sealed container.

TIP

Dress the salad with vinaigrette before adding it to the sandwiches. Stir together 1 tsp finely chopped shallot with 1 tsp white wine vinegar; 1½ tbsp extra virgin olive oil; a pinch each of salt, pepper and sugar; and ¼ tsp Dijon mustard.

Makes 2
Preparation: 20 minutes
+ 1 hour cooking time
+ 12 hours infusing time

BARBECUE "PULLED" JACKFRUIT SANDWICH

The classic street food sandwich, with spicy veggies and barbecue sauce, makes a delicious, healthy lunch. The role of "pulled pork" is played by jackfruit—a popular ingredient in Asian cuisine.

1 Put the jackfruit into a colander, let it drain well, rinse under cold water, and let it drain once again. Carefully shred into rough pieces. Heat the oil in a pan and sauté the jackfruit for 3–4 minutes over medium heat, then season with salt. Peel and crush the garlic and sauté this briefly, too. Add the barbecue sauce, stir, then cover and leave to simmer over low heat for 1 hour. Give it a stir every so often and, if necessary, splash in some water. Season to taste with salt and pepper, remove from the stove and let infuse for 12 hours.

2 Briefly toast the sliced bread under the broiler or in the toaster, then spread with a little bit of barbecue sauce. Top 2 pieces of bread with 1 lettuce leaf each. Arrange the tomato, onion, and some jackfruit "pulled pork" on top, then drizzle with barbecue sauce. Top with the remaining lettuce leaves and cover with the other slices of bread. Wrap the sandwiches to take with you.

3 cups (560g) canned green jackfruit in water or brine (see Tip, below)
2 tbsp olive oil
sea salt
2 garlic cloves
½ cup (150g) vegan barbecue sauce, plus extra for the sandwich
freshly ground black pepper
4 slices of bread
4 lettuce leaves
1 tomato, sliced
1 small red onion, finely sliced

TIP

You can buy canned jackfruit in Asian grocery stores. It's really important for this recipe to get young, green jackfruit in water or brine, and not preserved in syrup!

TEMPEH MAYO BAGEL

If you have fond memories of the taste of tuna fish, you will love this bagel. The nori seaweed flakes contribute a similar flavor, with tempeh further complementing the overall effect. This fermented soy product is like a little health boost that shouldn't just be limited to the dishes of its country of origin: Indonesia. There's no limit to the creativity you can exercise when filling these bagels—but one thing is certain: a few colorful bean sprouts will always make it prettier and tastier.

For the tempeh mayo
7oz (200g) tempeh, in a block
½ celery stick
½ small onion
½ cup (130g) Vegan Mayonnaise (see p57)
1 tsp dried dill
2 tbsp lemon juice
sea salt
freshly ground black pepper
1 tsp Dijon mustard
1 tsp agave syrup
2 tsp nori seaweed flakes (from an Asian grocery store)

For the bagels
2 bagels
4 lettuce leaves (optional)
handful of bean sprouts (optional)

1 To make the salad, steam the tempeh over simmering water for 20–30 minutes. Let cool, then finely crumble with your fingers, or in a food processor. Chop the celery finely. Peel the onion and chop this finely, too.

2 Combine the celery, onion, Vegan Mayonnaise, dill, lemon juice, salt, pepper, mustard, agave syrup, and nori flakes in a bowl and mix well. Fold in the tempeh and let the salad infuse in an airtight container for 12 hours.

3 To finish, halve and toast the bagels. Lay 2 lettuce leaves on the lower halves, top with the tempeh salad and bean sprouts, then cover with the upper bagel halves.

HASH BROWN DELUXE SANDWICH

Hash browns are far more than just a traditional American breakfast food. In this recipe, we include them in a really chic sandwich with a fantastically flavorful dressing. It will work wonders on your lunch break.

1 To make the hash browns, peel and coarsely grate the potatoes, put them into a clean paper towel, and thoroughly squeeze out any liquid. Mix with the salt, pepper, and nutmeg in a bowl. Heat ½–1 tsp oil in a pan, add half the potato mixture, use a spatula to press it down into a thin layer, and fry over medium heat for 3–4 minutes. Once the edge is crispy, carefully turn the hash brown over and fry the other side until golden brown. Remove and set aside to drain on some paper towels. Do the same with the remaining oil (½–1 tsp) and the remaining grated potato.

2 To make the dressing, add the mayonnaise to a small bowl and mix with the cucumber relish, sea salt, paprika, garlic and onion powders, the vinegar, and a little more pepper, adjusting the quantities to taste.

3 Toast the rolls or sliced bread, as you prefer. Spread the lower halves of the rolls or 2 slices of toast with the dressing and top with the lettuce, tomato, pickled cucumbers, fried onions, and hash browns. Cover with the tops of the rolls, or the remaining toast slices.

For the hash browns
1lb 2oz (500g) potatoes
½ tsp sea salt
freshly ground black pepper
pinch of freshly grated nutmeg
1–2 tsp canola oil

For the dressing
2 tbsp Vegan Mayonnaise (see p57)
2 tbsp cucumber relish (from a jar)
½ tsp sea salt
½ tsp sweet smoked paprika
½ tsp garlic powder
½ tsp onion powder
½ tsp cider vinegar

For the sandwich
2 whole-wheat rolls, or 4 slices of whole-wheat bread
handful of salad leaves
1 tomato, sliced
1½ tbsp sweet and spicy pickles
2 tsp store-bought crispy fried onions

SWEET POTATO BURGERS
WITH BARBECUE SAUCE

It's hard to imagine a more satisfying and substantial meal than these sweet potato burgers with barbecue sauce! They will make you full and happy. This delicious patty made from sweet potatoes is mixed with an exciting combination of spices, all stacked up with crunchy vegetables.

For the patties
1 large sweet potato
sea salt
1 shallot
½ bunch of chives
pinch of freshly ground black
    pepper
½ tsp sweet smoked paprika
1 tbsp dried marjoram
pinch of ground cumin
pinch of ground allspice
1 tsp Dijon mustard
2 tbsp plain or gluten-free flour
½ cup (40g) fresh breadcrumbs
2½ tbsp canola oil

For the burgers
2 large burger buns
vegan barbecue sauce
handful of salad leaves
small piece of cucumber, sliced
1 tomato, sliced
handful of cilantro leaves

1 To make the patties, peel the sweet potato, chop into little pieces, and cook for 10–15 minutes in salted water, until tender. Drain in a colander. Peel and finely chop the shallot. Snip the chives finely. Use a potato masher to mash up the sweet potato with the shallot and chives in a large bowl until evenly combined. Stir in ½ tsp salt, pepper, paprika, marjoram, cumin, allspice, and mustard. Add the flour and mix everything thoroughly again.

2 Spread the breadcrumbs out on a plate. Shape 2 even patties from the potato mixture and coat in the breadcrumbs. Heat the oil in a pan and fry the patties over medium heat on both sides until golden brown. Remove from the pan and allow to drain on some paper towels.

3 Split the burger buns in half, toast them, and spread the cut surface with barbecue sauce. Top the lower halves with salad leaves, then a patty, cucumber, tomato slices, and some cilantro. If desired, add some extra barbecue sauce.

PITA BREADS WITH "EGG SALAD"

This is an oriental-inspired delicacy made with crispy smoked tofu, crunchy fresh cabbage, and spices—all the magic of 1,001 nights wrapped up in a flatbread.

1 To make the salad, cut the smoked tofu into very small cubes. Heat the oil in a pan and sauté the smoked tofu initially over high heat and then over medium heat until it is crisp and firm. Set aside.

2 Cut the plain firm tofu into ½in (1cm) cubes, then peel and finely chop the red onion. Slice the scallions into rings. Drain the chickpeas thoroughly in a colander. Combine the plain firm tofu, red onion, scallions, cabbage, and chickpeas in a bowl.

3 Stir in the mayonnaise. Season the salad to be as spicy as you like using the black salt (if using), salt, pepper, curry powder, and turmeric. Fold in the smoked tofu and chopped chives. Open up the pita pockets. Package up the bread and salad separately, then fill the pitas with the salad when you are ready to eat.

5½oz (150g) smoked tofu
3 tbsp olive oil
9oz (250g) plain firm tofu
1 small red onion
2 scallions
⅓ cup (90g) canned chickpeas
2 cups (175g) green cabbage
½–¾ cup (150–200g) Vegan Mayonnaise (see p57)
1 slightly heaped tsp black salt *kala namak* (optional)
1½ tsp sea salt
½ tsp freshly ground black pepper
3 tsp curry powder
1 tbsp ground turmeric
1 tbsp chopped chives
2 pita breads

TIP Your lunch will be even tastier if you warm the flatbreads briefly in the oven just before filling.

Makes 4
Preparation: 40 minutes

For the kofta
½ cup (125g) red lentils
½ cup (120ml) vegetable stock
1 tbsp whole-wheat breadcrumbs
2 tbsp all-purpose flour
pinch of sea salt
pinch of hot paprika
pinch of smoked paprika
1 tbsp scallions, sliced
   into rings
olive oil, for frying

For the hummus
¾ cup (200g) canned chickpeas
juice of 1 small lemon
½ cup (100g) frozen spinach, thawed
3½ tbsp extra virgin olive oil
2 tsp tahini
1 tsp ground cumin
1 tsp sea salt
½ tsp curry powder
pinch of chili powder
2 small garlic cloves, crushed

For the sandwiches
4 small cherry tomatoes
1 large focaccia
2 handfuls of mixed salad leaves
1 small red pepper, sliced

FOCACCIA
WITH SPINACH HUMMUS AND RED LENTIL KOFTA

1 To make the lentil kofta, simmer the lentils in the stock over medium heat in a covered pan for 10–15 minutes, until soft.

2 Meanwhile, to make the hummus, drain the chickpeas and add them to a bowl with all the other hummus ingredients. Use a handheld blender to purée everything until smooth and creamy. Set aside.

3 Drain the lentils in a strainer and allow to cool slightly, then purée thoroughly with a handheld blender. Put them in a bowl and add the breadcrumbs, flour, salt, both types of paprika, and scallions and work everything together to a firm consistency. Use your hands to shape about 16 little balls from the mixture. Heat the oil for frying in a pan and cook the kofta in batches over medium heat, turning, until brown all over. Let drain on some paper towels.

4 Either halve or quarter the tomatoes, depending on size. Spilt the bread into 4 sections and, if desired, warm it in the oven, then slice each section open horizontally. Distribute the hummus, salad leaves, peppers, tomatoes, and 4 lentil kofta between each of the bread quarters.

TIP

Roasted garlic also works well with these sandwiches. Preheat the oven to 350°F (180°C), cut the stalk end from 1 small bulb of garlic, and peel off the outer skin. Mix 3 tbsp olive oil with 1 tsp herbes de Provence and a pinch of sea salt. Brush a heatproof dish with oil, put in the garlic, drizzle the rest of the oil over it, and bake for 30 minutes, until soft. Squeeze out the garlic cloves and use to stuff the sandwich.

VEGETABLE WRAPS

Savoy cabbage is wrapped around tempeh here, with a bit of shredded red cabbage for crunch and segments of orange for juicy zest. These little rolls are a great, refreshing alternative to the usual soggy and uninspiring doughy wraps you can buy in stores. Pack the dressing separately for dipping your rolls.

1 Wash the Savoy cabbage leaves and cut out the thick central stalks. Heat the stock in a pan and blanch the leaves over medium heat for 2 minutes. Take them out and plunge them in cold water, then pat them dry and set aside.

2 Slice the tempeh into thin strips. Peel the onion and slice finely. Heat the oil in a pan and sauté the tempeh strips over high heat. Add the sliced onion and continue to sauté until transparent. Season with salt and pepper.

3 Transfer the red cabbage to a bowl. Sprinkle with salt and then toss thoroughly. Peel and segment the orange, reserving any juice that comes out as you do so. Mix the orange segments and juice with the red cabbage. Fold in the chives.

4 To make the dressing, stir the soy yogurt in a bowl with the parsley, oil, salt, pepper, and cinnamon. Spread out the cabbage leaves on your work surface and put a bit of the red cabbage salad and tempeh along the center of each. Fold the sides of the leaves over the filling and then carefully roll up from the bottom. Finally, tie them up with string so that the rolls don't come apart while you are transporting them. Wrap them in foil or plastic wrap for your lunchbox. Pack the dressing separately.

For the wraps
4 large Savoy cabbage leaves
1 cup (250ml) vegetable stock
1¾oz (50g) tempeh
1 small red onion
1 tsp coconut oil
sea salt
freshly ground white pepper
1 cup (100g) red cabbage, cut
    into strips
½ orange
1 tbsp chopped chives

For the dressing
⅓ cup (100g) soy yogurt, or other
    plant-based yogurt
½ tbsp chopped parsley leaves
dash of walnut oil
pinch of sea salt
pinch of freshly ground white
    pepper
pinch of ground cinnamon

ASIAN
GLASS NOODLE SALAD WRAPS

It's glass noodle salad with a twist: packaged up in a delicious wrap. The filling provides everything you could want from the perfect glass noodle salad, enhanced with some added cashews. The end result is an East Asian delicacy in your lunchbox.

1 Slice the zucchini into spaghetti-like strips with a spiralizer. Alternatively, use a potato peeler to create thin slices lengthwise and then cut these into thin strips with a knife. Allow the zucchini and the noodles to soak in a large bowl of warm water for 10 minutes, until the noodles are soft. Transfer to a strainer and let the noodles and zucchini drain, before returning them to the bowl. Set aside.

2 Slice the scallions and onion thinly. Quarter the pepper, remove the seeds, and cut into thin strips. Peel and finely chop the garlic and ginger. Toast the cashew nuts in a dry frying pan until golden brown.

3 Heat the oil in a pan. Sauté the scallions, onion, and pepper over high heat. Add the garlic and ginger and continue to cook briefly. Pour in the soy sauce and coconut milk and add the cilantro. Fold in the cashew nuts.

4 Mix the pan of vegetables with the zucchini and glass noodle mixture in the bowl and add salt, pepper, and lime juice to taste. Divide the iceberg lettuce into individual leaves and shred slightly. Briefly heat the wraps and lay them out on your work surface. Spread sweet and sour sauce on them, top with lettuce leaves and the glass noodle salad, then roll them up firmly. Wrap in parchment paper, aluminum foil, or plastic wrap to take with you.

1 zucchini
2½oz (75g) glass noodles
½ bunch of scallions
½ onion
1 red pepper
1 small garlic clove
½in (1cm) piece of fresh ginger
¾oz (20g) cashew nuts
2½ tbsp sunflower oil
2 tbsp soy sauce
3½ tbsp coconut milk
1 tbsp chopped cilantro leaves
sea salt
freshly ground black pepper
1½ tbsp lime juice
¼ head iceberg lettuce
2 wraps
1½ tbsp vegan sweet and
   sour sauce

TIP Roll a wrap in a piece of parchment paper and cut it through diagonally. It looks really professional and is easier to eat without making a mess!

For 2 large wraps
Preparation: 30 minutes

SPINACH TOFU SCRAMBLE WRAP
WITH ARUGULA

Who needs eggs when you've got tofu? This is a kind of nondairy version of scrambled eggs that works wonderfully in this wrap with the accompanying spinach and crunchy red pepper. Neatly rolled up, it is the perfect lunch to pack up and take away.

For the spinach
1 small onion
1 garlic clove
½ tbsp vegan margarine
½ cup (100g) frozen spinach, defrosted
1 tbsp oat cream, or other plant-based cream

For the tofu scramble
1 small onion
1 large tomato
½ red pepper
9oz (250g) tofu
3 tbsp olive oil
¾ tsp ground turmeric
1½ tsp curry powder
2 tbsp soy sauce
2 tbsp soy milk, or other plant-based milk
sea salt
freshly ground black pepper
2 tbsp chopped chives

For the wraps
2 large wraps
2 cups (40g) arugula

1 To make the spinach mixture, peel the onion and garlic, then chop the onion and crush the garlic. Melt the margarine in a pan and sauté the onion over medium heat. Add the spinach and let it wilt with the lid on. Stir in the cream and garlic and let everything thicken slightly.

2 To make the tofu scramble, peel and chop the onion. Halve the tomato, remove the stalk and seeds, and chop the flesh. Seed and chop up the pepper. Crumble the tofu with your fingers. Heat the oil in a pan and fry the onion and tofu crumbs over high heat for 1 minute, then reduce the heat to medium and continue to fry until golden brown. Turn the mixture, add the turmeric and curry powder, and continue to cook everything for 3–4 more minutes. Pour in the soy sauce and cook for an additional 3–4 minutes. Next add the tomato and soy milk. Season everything to taste with salt and pepper and let it simmer gently for a bit longer. Remove the pan from the heat and finally fold the chives into the mixture.

3 To assemble, warm the wraps and lay them out on a work surface. Spread the spinach along the center of each wrap and top with the tofu scramble and some arugula. Fold the left and right sides of the wrap over the filling. Then, fold up the lower half, press down lightly, and firmly roll up the wrap from the lower edge. If desired, cut each wrap in half and wrap in aluminum foil to take with you.

Makes 1 large or
2 small burritos
Preparation: 15 minutes
+ 15 minutes cooking time

RICE AND BEAN BURRITOS
WITH SALSA

1 To make the rice, heat the oil in a pan and sauté the rice over medium heat. Add about ½ cup (130ml) water, the salsa, and salt. Bring to a boil over high heat, then cover, reduce the heat to a simmer, and cook for 10–15 minutes until done.

2 In the meantime, peel and finely chop the onion. Drain the beans in a colander. Heat the 2 tbsp of oil in a pan and sauté the onion and beans over high heat. Reduce the heat to medium and add the garlic and onion powders, salt, and sriracha sauce to taste. Pour in ¼ cup (80ml) water and let everything simmer for 2–3 minutes. Mash the bean mixture with a potato masher to produce a lumpy purée. If it seems too dry, add a little more water. Adjust the seasoning again.

3 Remove the pit and peel from the avocado half and slice it. Warm the tortilla, or tortillas, and lay it on your work surface. Spread the rice in a thick layer in the center and top with the beans. Lay avocado segments on top and drizzle over sriracha sauce before scattering with parsley. Fold the left and right sides of the tortilla over the filling. Then, fold up the lower half and press down lightly before rolling up firmly from the lower edge. If you like, you can heat a bit of oil in a pan and fry the burrito over high heat; this will help it hold together and add flavor. Wrap in aluminum foil and pack up for lunch.

For the rice
1 tbsp olive oil
1 cup (100g) jasmine rice
⅓ cup (100g) vegan hot salsa
½ tsp sea salt

For the beans
½ onion
¾ cup (200g) canned kidney beans
2 tbsp olive oil, plus extra for frying
½ tsp garlic powder
½ tsp onion powder
pinch of sea salt
sriracha sauce, to taste (or another kind of chili sauce)
½ avocado
1 very large (see Tip, below) or 2 small tortillas
parsley for sprinkling (optional)

TIP You can find a wide variety of sizes of flour and corn tortillas at your local Mexican grocery store. In place of sriracha sauce, you can also look for other vegan hot sauces there.

Makes 5
Preparation: 30 minutes
+ 30 minutes steaming time

For the vegan sausages
1⅓ cups (160g) gluten powder,
    or gluten flour
3 tsp fine oat flakes
¼ cup (20g) chickpea flour
1 tsp hot paprika
1 tsp smoked paprika
2 tbsp nutritional yeast flakes
2 tsp garlic powder
¾ tsp sea salt
½ tsp freshly ground black pepper
5oz (140g) medium firm tofu
⅓ cup (100ml) vegetable stock
2 tbsp olive oil, plus extra for frying
2 tbsp soy sauce

For the hotdogs
5 hotdog rolls
tomato ketchup
10 large dill pickle slices
toppings: mustard, Vegan
    Mayonnaise (see p57), fried
    onions (all optional)

Makes 5
Preparation: 20 minutes

For the curry sauce
1 large onion
5 tbsp olive oil
½ cup (160g) tomato ketchup
⅓ cup (100ml) vegetable stock
4 heaped tsp mild curry powder,
    plus extra to serve
½ tsp chili powder
sea salt
freshly ground black pepper
1 heaped tsp sugar

For the sausages
5 Vegan Sausages (see above)

HOMEMADE HOTDOGS

1 To make the sausages, mix together the gluten powder or flour, oat flakes, chickpea flour, hot paprika, smoked paprika, yeast flakes, garlic powder, salt, and pepper in a bowl. Purée the tofu, stock, oil, and soy sauce in a food processor until smooth. Add this paste to the flour mixture in the bowl and swiftly knead everything together. Split the mixture into 5 portions and shape each into a roughly 6in (15cm) long sausage.

2 Wrap up each of the sausages tightly in aluminum foil, twisting the ends together. Lay these packets in a steamer and cook over simmering water for 30 minutes. Let cool and unwrap from the foil. Heat a little oil in a frying pan and sauté the sausages over medium heat for 4–5 minutes, turning to brown all over.

3 To serve, heat the hotdog rolls and fill each with some ketchup, 1 sausage, and 2 slices of pickle. If you like, drizzle over some mustard or Vegan Mayonnaise and sprinkle with fried onions.

HOMEMADE CURRYWURST

1 Make the sausages following steps 1 and 2 above. To make the curry sauce, peel and finely chop the onion. Heat the oil in a pan and sauté the onion over medium heat. Add the ketchup and stock. Reduce the heat, stir in the curry powder, chili powder, salt, pepper, and sugar and let everything simmer gently.

2 To serve, cut the sausages into bite-sized pieces, drizzle with curry sauce, and dust with curry powder.

 TIP The sausages freeze well or can be kept in the fridge for 2—3 days.

Makes 4
Preparation: 20 minutes
+ 30 minutes rising time
+ 20 minutes cooking time

HERB, OLIVE, AND TOMATO FILLED
HOMEMADE ROLLS

These are the perfect finger food: homemade rolls with a Mediterranean-style filling baked inside. Loads of herbs balance a spectacular, rich mixture of tofu, tomatoes, and olives. Dig right in and enjoy—this is what is known as the ideal lunch.

For the dough
3 cups (400g) bread flour
1 tsp sea salt
¼oz (7g) packet of active dried yeast
1½ tbsp granulated sugar
1 tsp mixed seeds (such as poppy
    seed, or caraway seed for flavor)
1–2 tbsp crushed linseeds, plus
    1½ tbsp for sprinkling
3½ tbsp olive oil
2 tbsp soy cream, or other plant-
    based cream
1 tsp herbes de Provençe

For the filling
1 shallot
6oz (175g) basil tofu, or tofu rosso,
    or a mixture
1 tsp dried basil
1 tsp herbes de Provençe
½ tsp dried oregano
½ tsp sea salt
pinch of freshly ground black
    pepper
5 sun-dried tomatoes in oil
1 tbsp olive oil
2½ tbsp soy cream, or other
    plant-based cream
15 pitted Kalamata olives

1 To make the dough, mix together the flour, salt, active dried yeast, sugar, and seeds in a bowl using a whisk. Add the oil and ¾ cup (200ml) lukewarm water and knead everything by hand for about 10 minutes until you have a smooth dough, kneading vigorously to get lots of air into it. Cover and let rise in a warm place for 30 minutes.

2 Meanwhile, peel and roughly chop the shallot. Purée the shallot in a food processor with the tofu, basil, herbes de Provençe, oregano, salt, pepper, and sun-dried tomatoes. Then add the olive oil and soy cream and work everything to a spreadable texture which is not too crumbly. Depending on how large they are, either halve or quarter the olives and fold them into the mixture. If necessary, adjust the seasoning to taste with extra salt and pepper.

3 Preheat the oven to 400°F (200°C). Line a baking sheet with parchment paper. Split the dough into 4 equal-sized pieces and press each piece by hand into a flat disc. Place one-quarter of the filling on each disc, fold over the edges of the dough, press firmly together, and smooth out slightly. Turn the roll over and reshape the upper surface to make it neater.

4 Place the bread rolls on the parchment paper, brush liberally with soy cream, and sprinkle with linseed and herbes de Provençe. Bake for about 18 minutes in the center of the oven. Allow to cool completely on a wire rack.

Makes a 10in (25cm) loaf
Preparation: 10 minutes
+ 30 minutes rising time
+ 1 hour cooking time

ZUCCHINI BREAD

Feel like taking bread to work for a snack? Try this special bread! With zucchini, carrot, and exquisite macadamia nuts, this vitamin-rich loaf is the ideal companion when you're out and about. And it's really versatile, too: you can spread it with either sweet or spicy toppings. It's great with whatever flavor you are craving.

1 Grate the zucchini and carrot. Chop the nuts and mix them with the flour, salt, cinnamon, baking powder, sugar, and lemon juice in a bowl. Add the zucchini and carrot followed by ⅔ cup (150ml) water and stir until everything is combined evenly. Cover and let the mixture rise for about 30 minutes.

2 Preheat the oven to 350°F (180°C). Grease the pan, pour in the mixture, and bake in the lower part of the oven for about 1 hour. Test the loaf by inserting a wooden toothpick into the center. If there is no mixture sticking to it when you pull it out, the bread is ready; if there is, bake it for a few minutes more, then test again. Let cool in the pan for 10 minutes, then turn out onto a wire rack and allow to cool completely.

1 large or 2 small zucchini
1 small carrot
2½oz (75g) macadamia nuts
2 cups (225g) all-purpose flour
pinch of sea salt
pinch of ground cinnamon
1 tsp baking powder
½ cup (80g) granulated sugar
juice of ½ lemon
vegan margarine, for the pan

Special equipment
10in (25cm) long loaf pan

TIP For a sweeter version, stir together ½ cup (75g) powdered sugar and 2 tbsp lemon juice to make a glaze and pour it over the loaf; or brush the top with melted vegan chocolate and sprinkle with chopped nuts. Kids love this bread, sliced, with jam and peanut butter. For a savory version, spread a slice of the bread with a savory spread (see pp90—94) and eat it with lettuce, cucumber, and tomatoes.

SATISFYING MAINS

hearty and filling—vegetables, pasta, & rice

Makes 1 large or 2 small portions
Preparation: 15 minutes

MEDITERRANEAN
STUFFED TOMATOES

Really ripe tomatoes are used in this little feast, which can be quickly rustled up for your everyday lunchbox. The tomatoes are stuffed with a creamy filling whisked together from homemade cashew cheese, nondairy cream, nutritious argan oil, arugula, and black olives—all of which are packed full of flavor. Pop the lids on and they're ready!

4 tomatoes
3 cups (60g) arugula
6 pitted black olives
½ cup (100g) Hot Cashew "Cream Cheese" (see p94)
2 tbsp spelt cream, or other plant-based cream
½ tsp argan oil
pinch of sea salt
pinch of freshly ground black pepper
pinch of dried oregano
pinch of dried rosemary

1 Cut a little lid off the stalk-end of each tomato. Hollow out the tomatoes using a spoon, discard the seeds, and chop the flesh. Chop the arugula very finely. Chop the olives.

2 Use a handheld blender to purée the Hot Cashew "Cream Cheese," cream, and oil. Fold in the chopped tomatoes, arugula, and olives, then season to taste with salt, pepper, oregano, and rosemary. Distribute the mixture between the hollowed-out tomatoes. Replace the tomato lids. This dish tastes great with some rustic bread.

Makes 1 large or 2 small portions
Preparation: 25 minutes

EGGPLANT SCHNITZEL
WITH GARLIC CREAM

Absolutely ravenous? Craving something really filling? These eggplants with their crisp and spicy paprika-and-oat coating are just the thing and certainly a far cry from the usual dull lunchtime fare. The garlic cream is super-quick to prepare and is wonderful for greedy dipping! This excellent main course scores high on the pleasure scale.

1 To make the schnitzel, chop off both ends of the eggplant. Cut it lengthwise into ¾in (2cm) thick slices. Salt the slices on both sides, lay them on a thick layer of paper towels, weigh them down with a chopping board, and leave for 10 minutes to remove the liquid from the vegetable.

2 Meanwhile, spread the flour onto a flat plate (reserving 1 tbsp) and season with salt and pepper. Gradually stir the remaining flour (1 tbsp) into the cold cream. Season the cream with salt, 1 tsp pepper, paprika, and yeast flakes. Spread the panko breadcrumbs on another plate.

3 Pat dry the slices of eggplant. First coat the slices in the flour, then draw them through the cream, and finally dredge them in the panko breadcrumbs. Heat the oil in a pan and sauté the eggplant schnitzel in batches over medium heat until golden brown on both sides. Let them drain on a wire rack.

4 To make the cream, peel and finely chop the garlic and stir it into the Vegan Mayonnaise. Package up the schnitzels and cream separately to take with you. The schnitzels taste great either warm or cold. Serve with a crispy flatbread and/or a crunchy salad with a great dressing (see pp56–57).

For the schnitzel
1 large eggplant
sea salt
1 cup (100g) all-purpose flour
freshly ground white pepper
1 cup (200g) chilled oat cream,
    or other plant-based cream
½ tsp sweet smoked paprika
2 tsp yeast flakes
1 cup (100g) panko or breadcrumbs
3½ tbsp olive oil

For the garlic cream
1 garlic clove
½ cup (100g) Vegan Mayonnaise
    (see p57)

BAKED SWEET POTATOES
WITH LENTIL AND AVOCADO SALAD AND A GRAPEFRUIT DIP

If you are a bit adventurous, this recipe will be right up your alley. Baked sweet potatoes are served with a lentil and avocado salad, and the whole thing is topped with a dip made from vegan cream cheese, grapefruit, and spices.

For the sweet potatoes and salad
2 small sweet potatoes
¾ cup (150g) beluga lentils
½ cup (100ml) vegetable stock
1 avocado (ideally the Hass variety)
1 small red onion
½ red chile
1 tbsp white wine vinegar
2 tbsp extra virgin olive oil
sea salt
freshly ground black pepper

For the dip
½ cup (100g) vegan cream cheese
finely grated zest and juice of
    ¼ unwaxed grapefruit
pinch of cayenne pepper
pinch of red pepper flakes

1 Preheat the oven to 400°F (200°C). Wash and pat dry the sweet potatoes, prick with a fork, place on a baking sheet lined with aluminum foil, and bake in the center of the oven for 25 minutes.

2 Meanwhile, cook the lentils in the stock according to the package instructions until they are just done. Halve the avocado and remove the pit. Scoop out the avocado from the skin using a spoon and chop it finely. Peel and finely chop the onion. Seed and finely chop the chile. Drain the lentils in a strainer, then mix in a bowl with the avocado, onion, and chile. Stir together the vinegar, oil, salt, and pepper to make the dressing. Pour the dressing over the lentils and gently stir to coat them.

3 For the dip, mix the cream cheese with the grapefruit zest and juice, cayenne pepper, and red pepper flakes, and stir until smooth. Season with salt and pepper to taste.

4 Pack up the sweet potatoes (wrapped in aluminum foil), salad, and dip separately to take with you. To serve, optionally reheat the potatoes and cut them lengthwise, or split into halves. Top with the salad and serve with the dip.

Makes 1 large or 2 small portions
Preparation: 35 minutes
+ 30 minutes infusing time

GRILLED
MINI PEPPERS
WITH RAINBOW BULGUR

These little peppers are called Padrón peppers, and they originate from Galicia in Spain. They can be baked in the oven and are a delight to eat, not just with this colorful bulgur salad, but also on their own. This beautiful dish is enhanced with a Middle Eastern-style dressing.

1 Preheat the oven to 400°F (200°C). Wash the Padrón peppers, pat them dry with paper towels, and lay them in a single layer in a heatproof dish. Drizzle with oil and season with salt and pepper. Chop the rosemary (if using), and scatter over the peppers. Bake in the center of the oven for 20 minutes.

2 Meanwhile, peel and finely chop the onion for the bulgur salad. Heat the oil in a pan and sauté the onion and bulgur over medium heat. Pour in the stock, stir everything well, and let the bulgur swell by leaving it, covered, over low heat for around 10 minutes. Remove the pan from the stove and allow to cool.

3 Trim the scallions and slice finely. Quarter the yellow pepper, remove the seeds, and chop it into bite-sized pieces. Halve the tomatoes. Finely chop the dates and the parsley.

4 To make the dressing, stir together all the ingredients in a little bowl. Mix the bulgur with the scallions, yellow pepper, tomatoes, dates, parsley, and the dressing. To serve, lay the Padrón peppers on the bulgur, or serve alongside. This is perfect for preparing the evening before, as the flavor of the bulgur improves the longer it marinates in the dressing.

For the peppers
2 cups (300g) Padrón peppers
2 tbsp olive oil
sea salt
freshly ground black pepper
sprig of rosemary (optional)

For the bulgur
1 small onion
1 tbsp oil
1 cup (80g) bulgur wheat
1 cup (250ml) vegetable stock
½ bunch of scallions
1 large yellow pepper
3 cherry tomatoes
5 pitted dates
3–4 sprigs of flat leaf parsley

For the dressing
finely grated zest and juice of
  ½ small unwaxed lemon
1½ tbsp argan oil
1 tsp light balsamic vinegar
1 tsp tomato purée
½ tsp harissa
½ tsp ras el hanout
1 tsp agave syrup

LITTLE QUINOA BALLS
WITH MINT SAUCE

These golden spheres are not just visually delightful, they are also rich in healthy protein. The refreshing mint and yogurt sauce, with its delicate hint of lemon, adds the perfect finishing touch to this unbelievably delicious dish, which can be enjoyed either warm or cold.

For the quinoa balls

1 cup (150g) quinoa
¾ cup (225ml) vegetable stock
1 small onion
1 small red pepper
½ bunch of scallions
1 tbsp olive oil, plus extra for frying
1 cup (125g) whole-wheat
    breadcrumbs
2 tsp gluten-free flour, or other
    flour
½ tsp herb salt, or sea salt plus
    ½ tsp mixed herbs
pinch of ground Indian Tellicherry
    peppercorns, or black pepper
½ tsp curry powder
pinch of sugar

For the sauce

3 sprigs of mint
1 garlic clove (optional)
finely grated zest and juice of
    ½ small unwaxed lemon
¾ cup (200g) soy yogurt, or other
    plant-based yogurt
sea salt
freshly ground white pepper

1 Rinse the quinoa in a strainer until the water runs clear. Bring it to a boil in the stock and simmer over medium heat until the quinoa has absorbed the stock. In the meantime, peel and finely chop the onion. Quarter the pepper, remove the seeds, and chop into little cubes. Trim the scallions and slice into fine rings. Heat the 1 tbsp oil in a sauté pan and sauté the onion, pepper, and scallions over medium heat until transparent. Let cool slightly.

2 For the sauce, pick the leaves from the mint stalks and chop finely. Peel and finely chop the garlic, if using. Stir together the mint, garlic, lemon zest and juice, and yogurt until smooth. Season with salt and pepper.

3 Mix together the quinoa, vegetable mixture, breadcrumbs, flour, and herb salt. Add the pepper, curry powder, and sugar and combine everything well. Use your hands to shape the mixture into little balls (see Tip, below). Heat some oil in a pan and fry the little balls over medium heat until they are golden brown all over. Remove from the pan and allow to drain on some paper towels. Pack up the little balls and the sauce separately to take with you—they taste great warm or cold. Naan breads or salad go really well with these.

 TIP
The easiest way to shape these balls is with slightly dampened hands. Try to make the balls nice and round and about the size of a golf ball.

STUFFED POLENTA
WITH GREEN MOJO

1 To make the filling, put the soy chunks in a bowl, pour over the stock, and let soak for 5 minutes. Drain in a colander and allow to cool slightly. Use your hands to squeeze out as much of the liquid as possible.

2 In a small bowl, mix together the marjoram, thyme, hot and sweet paprika, parsley, oregano, nutmeg, onion powder, and salt. Add 4 tbsp of the olive oil and stir everything together to create a thin paste. Spread this paste over the soy chunks and work together using your hands. Set aside.

3 To make the polenta, bring the stock and soy milk to a boil in a large saucepan. Add the polenta, stirring all the time until you have a smooth mixture. Stir in the margarine. Switch off the heat, cover, and leave the polenta to swell for 10 minutes.

4 In the meantime, preheat the oven to 350°F (180°C). To finish off preparing the filling, heat 2 tbsp more olive oil in a pan and sauté the soy chunks over high heat. Set aside and allow to cool. Halve the zucchini, then cut into thin slices. Quarter the pepper, remove the seeds, and chop into cubes.

5 Season the polenta very generously, divide between four 16in (40cm) squares of foil, and spread it out slightly. Top each with one-quarter of the vegetables, tomatoes, and the soy chunks. Drizzle with the remaining 2 tbsp of oil. Close each piece of foil to create a packet or roll so that the polenta is folded up over the filling and no air can escape. Lay the packets on a baking sheet and bake in the center of the oven for around 30 minutes.

6 Meanwhile, make the mojo sauce. Roughly chop the parsley. Use a food processor to purée the parsley, cumin, oil, lemon juice, and a little salt to a smooth consistency. Pack up the polenta packets and the mojo separately to take with you.

For the filling
2½oz (75g) coarse soy chunks (from a health food store)
1 cup (250ml) hot vegetable stock
1 tsp dried marjoram
1 tsp dried thyme
½ tsp hot paprika
½ tsp sweet paprika
pinch of dried parsley
pinch of dried oregano
pinch of freshly grated nutmeg
1 tsp onion powder
sea salt
8 tbsp olive oil
1 small zucchini
1 red pepper
12 cherry tomatoes

For the polenta
¾ cup (200ml) vegetable stock
¾ cup (200ml) soy milk, or other plant-based milk
1½ cups (200g) fine polenta cornmeal
1 tbsp vegan margarine
freshly ground black pepper

For the mojo
small bunch of curly parsley
1 tsp ground cumin
⅔ cup (150ml) extra virgin olive oil
squeeze of lemon juice

Makes 1 large or 2 small
portions
Preparation: 20 minutes
+ 15 minutes cooking time

POTATO "RISOTTO"

Sometimes it's good to do things a bit differently—this lunchbox risotto is made from potatoes instead of rice. The olives, capers, and sun-dried tomatoes provide a culinary lunchtime escape to the Mediterranean—dreaming about your dream vacation while you eat is definitely encouraged!

14oz (400g) new potatoes
1 small red pepper
1 shallot
1 small garlic clove
2 tbsp olive oil
3 tbsp vegan margarine
3 tbsp capers, rinsed
1¼oz (40g) pitted black olives
½ cup (50g) sun-dried tomatoes
   in oil
2 tbsp white wine
1 tsp balsamic vinegar
1¾ cups (400ml) vegetable stock
sea salt
freshly ground black pepper
pinch of dried basil
pinch of dried rosemary
pinch of dried thyme
pinch of sugar
2 tbsp chopped chives

1 Peel the potatoes and cut into small cubes. Quarter the pepper, remove the seeds, and chop into small cubes. Peel and finely chop the shallot and garlic.

2 Heat the oil and margarine in a sauté pan and sauté the potatoes, pepper, shallot, and garlic over medium heat. Finely chop the capers, olives, and tomatoes, add them to the pan, and cook briefly. Deglaze with the wine and vinegar, scraping at the base of the pan, then pour in the stock and cook, stirring, for 15 minutes.

3 Season with salt, pepper, the herbs, and sugar, and fold in the chopped chives. Place into a lunchbox to take with you.

SWEETCORN FRITTATAS
WITH MANGO CHUTNEY

Sweet meets spicy, with crispy baked sweetcorn and a sweetly refreshing and tart mango chutney. Subtle hints of chili and ginger add a bit of extra spice to this delicious and filling combination.

1 To make the frittatas, grate the zucchini finely and mix in a bowl with ½ tsp salt. Let drain in a colander. Similarly, drain the sweetcorn, put this in a bowl, too, and crush some of the kernels roughly with a fork.

2 Mix the cornflour, chickpea flour, and baking soda in a bowl using a whisk. Stir together the stock, tomato purée, and scallion greens, and add this to the flour mixture. Squeeze as much liquid as you can out of the zucchini before adding it to the flour mixture with the sweetcorn. Work everything together to create a doughlike consistency. Season with salt and pepper and divide into 6 portions. Shape each into a small, flat cake. Heat the oil in a pan and fry the frittatas in batches over medium heat until golden brown on both sides. Allow to drain on paper towels.

3 Peel the mango to make the chutney. Remove the pit and finely chop the fruit. Peel the onion and ginger and chop finely. Heat the oil in a small pan and sauté the onion over medium heat, then add the ginger and continue to cook briefly. Add the mango, vinegar, sugar, curry powder, lemon juice, chili powder, and 2 tbsp water, and simmer for about 5 minutes, stirring continuously until the mixture is slightly mushy, but still with distinct chunks of fruit. Pour into a warm, clean screw-top jar, seal firmly, and allow to cool. Pack up the frittatas and chutney separately to take with you. The frittatas taste great either warm or cold.

For the frittatas
1 zucchini
sea salt
½ cup (100g) canned sweetcorn
⅓ cup (40g) cornflour
¾ cup (75g) chickpea flour
½ tsp baking soda
3½ tbsp vegetable stock
1 tbsp tomato purée
2 tbsp chopped scallion greens
freshly ground black pepper
olive oil

For the chutney
½ mango
1 red onion
1in (2.5cm) piece of fresh ginger
1 tbsp olive oil
2 tbsp white wine vinegar
2 tbsp brown sugar
1 tsp mild curry powder
2 tbsp lemon juice
pinch of chili powder, or to taste

 TIP The chutney tastes delicious with a few chopped mint leaves.

Makes 1 large or 2 small portions
Preparation: 25 minutes
+ 20 minutes cooking time

SPAGHETTI FRITTATAS

These little noodle nests are truly predestined for the lunchbox. Our spaghetti frittatas combine all the best features of a delicious, creamy pasta dish. They are baked until crisp to make them even tastier, and best of all, you can eat them with your fingers.

For the frittatas

5½oz (150g) whole-wheat spaghetti

sea salt

1oz (30g) smoked tofu

1 small onion

1oz (30g) pitted green olives

1 tbsp olive oil

4 tbsp soy cream, or other plant-based cream

½ cup (60g) vegan pizza cheese, shredded

pinch of herb salt, or sea salt plus a pinch of mixed herbs

freshly ground black pepper

pinch of dried oregano

vegan margarine, for the lunchbox

4 basil leaves, to garnish

1 Cook the spaghetti in salted water, according to the package instructions, until al dente. Meanwhile, cut the tofu into little cubes. Peel and finely chop the onion and olives.

2 Heat the oil in a large high-sided pan and sauté the tofu over high heat. Add the onion and olives and cook briefly. Pour in the cream and ¼ cup (30g) of the cheese. Season with herb salt, pepper, and oregano, and simmer over low heat until the cheese has melted.

3 Preheat the oven to 425°F (220°C). Grease 4 muffin pan molds with the margarine. Drain the spaghetti briefly in a colander, then mix with the cheese mixture. Distribute the pasta mix between the muffin molds; the best way to do this is to use a large fork to twist the spaghetti.

4 Scatter the remaining cheese over the spaghetti and bake the frittatas in the center of the oven for 20 minutes. Remove and let cool slightly before releasing from the molds. Pack them up and serve garnished with some basil leaves. The frittatas taste great either warm or cold.

SPAGHETTI POMODORI E OLIO

High-quality olive oil, delicate pine nuts, a hint of lemon, and juicy tomatoes are what make this classic dish so irresistible. Real Italian fare for your lunchbox—*buon gusto!*

1 Cook the spaghetti in salted water according to the package instructions until it is al dente. Meanwhile, quarter the tomatoes, remove the stalk and seeds, and chop finely. Peel and finely chop the garlic and parsley. Stir the oil together with 1 tbsp water and the stock. Combine the oil mixture with the tomatoes, garlic, and parsley, then add salt, pepper, lemon juice, and agave syrup.

2 Dry-roast the pine nuts in a pan until golden brown, then chop roughly. Drain the spaghetti in a colander, return to the hot pan, and put over medium heat. Fold in the tomato mixture and warm everything through for around 1 minute, stirring constantly. Transfer the spaghetti to your lunchbox and sprinkle with the pine nuts.

Makes 1 large or 2 small portions
Preparation: 25 minutes

5½oz (150g) whole-wheat spaghetti
sea salt
2 tomatoes
1 garlic clove
½ small bunch of flat leaf parsley
1 tbsp extra virgin olive oil
1 tsp powdered vegetable stock
freshly ground black pepper
squeeze of lemon juice
½ tsp agave syrup
2½ tbsp pine nuts

POTSTICKER NOODLES

So simple, so good: rice noodles, bok choy, and deliciously aromatic ginger, curry paste, and sesame oil all mingle splendidly in this Asian concoction. Broccoli joins the assembled ranks of delicious ingredients to add a nice crunch—and a lot of green nutrition—to the noodles.

For the sauce
5 tbsp soy sauce
1 tbsp rice vinegar
1 tbsp red curry paste
½ tsp sesame oil
pinch of chili powder
2 tbsp finely chopped scallion
   greens

For the noodles
½ small bok choy, about 1 cup, chopped
1 tbsp coconut oil
½ cup (80g) broccoli florets
sea salt
freshly ground black pepper
2¼oz (80g) broad rice noodles
   (from an Asian grocery store)
½ tsp finely grated fresh ginger

1 To make the sauce, add all the ingredients to a screw-top jar. Close the lid firmly and shake vigorously until the ingredients are well combined. Set aside.

2 Finely chop the bok choy. Heat the oil in a pan and sauté the broccoli until it is just cooked. Season with salt and pepper and set aside.

3 Cook the noodles in salted water according to the package instructions. Add the bok choy shortly before the end of the cooking time. Drain the noodles and bok choy in a colander, plunge into cold water, then drain again, and return to the pan. Add the sauce and heat everything through again. Fold in the broccoli and ginger, then transfer to your lunchbox.

TIP "Potstickers" are filled dumplings made from rice flour. For our "potsticker" pasta, the filling is simply mixed in with the rice noodles. It's quicker and easier, but just as tasty.

FRIED RICE
WITH PINEAPPLE AND CASHEW NUTS

Fruity pineapple, sweetcorn, and golden-brown toasted cashew nuts give this delicately bronzed jasmine rice everything it needs to be a truly memorable culinary experience.

1 Cook the rice in salted water according to the package instructions. Drain in a strainer and allow to cool. Toast the cashews in a small dry frying pan until golden brown, then remove from the heat and set aside. Chop the pineapple rings into bite-sized pieces. Melt the margarine in the pan over medium heat, sauté the pineapple, then set aside.

2 Halve the pepper, remove the seeds, then chop into small chunks. Peel the carrot and slice thinly using a vegetable peeler. Drain the sweetcorn in a colander. Heat 2 tbsp oil in a wok or frying pan. Sauté the pepper and carrot over high heat, then continue to cook over medium heat until golden brown and al dente. If the carrot browns too much before it is cooked, add a little water (any added liquid should evaporate completely). Season the vegetables with salt, pepper, and paprika.

3 Add the remaining 2 tbsp oil and increase the heat. Stir in the rice and sauté briefly over high heat until crisp, then continue to brown over medium heat. If the mixture dries out too much, add a little more oil. Fold in the sweetcorn, pineapple, and cashews and heat through. Transfer the rice dish to a lunchbox. Wash and slice the scallions and scatter them over the rice. Sprinkle with paprika.

½ cup (100g) jasmine rice
sea salt
2oz (60g) cashew nuts
2 canned pineapple rings
2 tbsp vegan margarine
1 small red pepper
1 carrot
⅓ cup (80g) canned sweetcorn
4 tbsp olive oil, plus extra if needed
good pinch of freshly ground
   white pepper
1½ tsp hot paprika, plus extra
   for sprinkling
2 scallions, green sections
   only

TIP

The recipe also tastes great with broccoli and flaked almonds —you can eat it warm or cold, and as leftovers the next day.

ARABIAN RICE

This is modeled after *kabsa*, an Arabian rice dish usually served with meat. In this recipe we use seitan instead, and it proves to be the perfect companion for the rice, Middle Eastern spices, and crunchy slivered almonds.

1⅓ cups (250g) long grain rice
1 carrot
½ red pepper
1 shallot
1 garlic clove
5½oz (150g) seitan
1½ tbsp olive oil
1 tsp tomato purée
finely grated zest and juice
    of ½ unwaxed orange
2 cups (500ml) vegetable stock,
    plus extra if needed
½ cup (50g) slivered almonds
½ tsp *pul biber* (Aleppo pepper,
    or Turkish chili flakes)
pinch of saffron threads
pinch of ground cinnamon
pinch of ground cumin
pinch of ground cardamom
sea salt
freshly ground black pepper
freshly grated nutmeg
handful of raisins (optional)

1 Put the rice in a strainer and rinse until the water runs clear. Leave to drain and set aside. Peel and finely chop the carrot. Quarter the pepper, remove the seeds, then finely chop. Peel and chop the shallot and garlic.

2 Chop the seitan into bite-sized pieces. Heat the oil in a pan and sauté the seitan over high heat on all sides. Stir in the tomato purée, carrot, pepper, shallot, garlic, and orange zest and juice. Add the rice, plus sufficient stock to cover the rice well. Simmer over medium heat for about 20 minutes until cooked, stirring occasionally and adding more stock if necessary.

3 Meanwhile, toast the slivered almonds in a dry pan. Season the rice with *pul biber*, saffron, cinnamon, cumin, and cardamom, and add a pinch each of salt, pepper, and nutmeg. Stir in the raisins (if using). Put into 2 lunchboxes and sprinkle with the almonds. If possible serve the *kabsa* hot, but the dish also tastes great served cold or at room temperature.

Makes 2 large portions
Preparation: 45 minutes

GREEK BOWLS

You really must try out these recipes at the same time if you can—all these Greek treats go well together. These gyros are made from soy chunks served with tzatziki in the traditional manner; delicious vine leaves, stuffed with a fresh lemony rice; and a little mezze bean side dish with the all-essential garlic and spices.

Makes 1 large portion
Preparation: 25 minutes
+ 12 hours infusing time
+ 30 minutes draining time

For the gyros
1⅓ cups (300ml) hot vegetable stock
2½oz (75g) coarse soy crumbs (from a health food store)
4 tbsp olive oil, plus more for frying
1 generously heaped tbsp gyros seasoning

For the tzatziki
½ cucumber
1 tsp sea salt
1 small garlic clove
⅓ cup (90g) soy yogurt, or other plant-based yogurt
1 tbsp extra virgin olive oil
1 tbsp lemon juice
½ tbsp dried dill
freshly ground black pepper

SOY GYROS WITH TZATZIKI

1 To make the gyros, pour the stock over the soy crumbs in a bowl and let steep for 10 minutes. Drain in a colander and allow to cool. Squeeze out the soy crumbs well and mix with the 4 tbsp oil and gyros seasoning in a bowl. Let infuse in a freezer bag or airtight container in the fridge for 12 hours.

2 Heat a generous amount of oil in a pan and fry the soy crumbs, initially over high heat, then continue to cook over lower heat until well browned all over. Set aside.

3 To make the tzatziki, halve the cucumber lengthwise, remove the seeds, and grate finely. Mix with the salt and alloq to drain in a colander for 30 minutes, then squeeze out thoroughly. Peel and crush the garlic. Combine the grated cucumber in a bowl with the garlic, yogurt, oil, lemon juice, and dill. Season to taste with pepper. Pack up the gyros and tzatziki separately to take with you. Reheat the gyros briefly before serving.

 TIP If you like, you can replace the dill in the tzatziki with finely chopped mint leaves.

STUFFED VINE LEAVES WITH LEMON RICE

1 Toast the pine nuts in a dry pan until golden brown, then chop finely and set aside. Peel and finely chop the onion. Heat 4 tbsp oil in a pan and sauté the onion over medium heat. Add the rice and fry briefly, then pour in half the stock and simmer over low heat for about 18 minutes, stirring frequently, and gradually adding the remaining stock during this time. Toward the end of the cooking time, stir in the lemon zest and juice and pine nuts.

2 Wash the vine leaves under cold running water and remove the stalks. Lay the leaves on your work surface with their rough sides facing upward. Put 1 heaped tbsp rice onto each and fold over the right and left sides of each leaf. Roll up the leaves firmly, starting at the stalk end. Lay the little rolls snugly together in a small pan. Drizzle with the remaining 4 tbsp oil, sprinkle with salt, and pour in water to cover. Weigh them down with a small plate, then cover, bring to a boil, and simmer over low heat for 25 minutes. Carefully remove the vine leaves and allow to cool. Serve with lemon slices.

Makes 12
Preparation: 35 minutes
+ 25 minutes cooking time

2½ tbsp pine nuts
1 small onion
8 tbsp olive oil
½ cup (100g) risotto rice
1⅓ cups (300ml) vegetable stock
finely grated zest and juice of
 1 unwaxed lemon plus extra
 lemon slices to serve
12 preserved vine leaves
1 tsp sea salt

TIP

While you are cooking, you might as well make a larger quantity—the vine leaves will keep, covered in olive oil, for several days.

MEZZE GREEN BEANS

1 Cut the ends off the beans. Cover with water in a pan and add the salt and bay leaf. Cook over medium heat for 5–8 minutes until al dente, then drain in a colander, blanch in cold water, and let drain.

2 Heat the oil in a pan and sauté the beans over high heat; continue to cook over medium heat until golden brown. Switch off the heat. Add the vinegar to the beans. Peel and crush the garlic over the beans. Mix everything well and let infuse slightly. Finally, season to taste with sea salt and pepper. Some crunchy fresh bread tastes great with this dish.

Makes 1 lunchbox
Preparation: 20 minutes
+ infusing time

9oz (250g) green beans
1½ tsp sea salt
1 bay leaf
2 tbsp olive oil
1 tbsp balsamic vinegar
2 garlic cloves
freshly ground black pepper

TIP The Arabic word mezze roughly translates as "small meal." Here, this consists of green beans which are given a wonderfully intense flavor by sautéing them briefly, then adding garlic, balsamic vinegar, and salt.

INDIAN VEGETABLE PANCAKES

These unbeatable little pancakes are made from semolina and vegetables. Served with a fruity mango chutney, they are a delicious meal for an Indian-inspired lunch break.

1 small onion
1 small red pepper
2 sprigs of cilantro
½ cup (80g) semolina
⅔ cup (150ml) cold vegetable stock
½ tsp sea salt
½ tsp curry powder
pinch of chili powder
pinch of ground cardamom
2 tbsp canola oil
1 tbsp cucumber relish
1½ cups (500g) Mango Chutney (see
    p139, or ready-made)

1 Peel and finely chop the onion. Cut the pepper into quarters, then chop into little cubes. Finely chop the cilantro. Stir together the semolina, stock, salt, curry powder, chili powder, and cardamom in a bowl. Add the chopped onion and pepper with the cilantro and stir until everything is combined.

2 Heat 1 tbsp oil in a pan. Add half the batter to the pan and spread out gently. Cook the pancake over medium heat for 2–3 minutes until slightly brown. Turn and cook for another 2–3 minutes. Add the remaining oil to the pan and cook the rest of the batter to make a second pancake. Stir together the cucumber relish and the mango chutney to make a dip. Pack up the pancakes and dip separately to take with you. To serve, spread the pancake with the dip—it tastes great either warm or cold.

TIP Try another Indian classic: red lentil pancakes. To make the batter, stir 1¼ cups (150g) ground red lentils with ¾ cup (170ml) water and season with 1 tsp garam masala, ½ tsp curry powder, and ½ tsp sea salt. Leave to steep for a good 15 minutes. Heat 2½ tbsp canola oil in a pan and cook little pancakes in batches over medium heat until golden brown. Mango chutney goes wonderfully with these, too.

Makes a 11in (28cm) quiche/
8 slices
Preparation: 15 minutes
+ 1 hour chilling time
+ 30 minutes cooking time

ASPARAGUS QUICHE

Quiche is wonderfully versatile. The pastry here is quick to make and all you need to do is put in the filling. This recipe combines green and white asparagus with tasty silken tofu and soy cream to create a really luxurious treat—instant pleasure in your lunchbox.

1 To make the pastry, put the flour and salt in a bowl and chop in the margarine. Briefly rub it together with your fingertips until the mixture resembles breadcrumbs. Sprinkle in the sugar and 8 tbsp water and stir with a knife until the mixture comes together in clumps and leaves the bowl clean. Form the pastry into a disc, wrap in plastic wrap, and leave for 1 hour in the fridge.

2 For the filling, chop the woody ends from both types of asparagus. Peel the lower one-third of the green asparagus spears. Cut the chile in half lengthwise, remove the seeds, then slice into narrow strips. Preheat the oven to 350°F (180°C). Grease a 11in (28cm) springform pan.

3 Roll out the pastry on a floured work surface until it is large enough to line the pan. Carefully roll it over the rolling pin and lay it in the pan, pushing down gently in the corners to form a pastry case. Stir together the tofu, cream, cornflour, oil, oregano, and basil in a bowl until you have a smooth, creamy consistency, then season to taste with salt and pepper. Spread the cream over the pastry, then arrange the different colored asparagus and the chile strips in an alternating pattern on top.

4 Bake the quiche in the center of the oven for 25–30 minutes until golden. Let it cool slightly in the pan on a wire rack. To serve or pack for lunch, remove the quiche from the pan and cut into pieces.

For the pastry
2½ cups (325g) all-purpose flour, plus extra for dusting
1 tsp sea salt
½ cup (150g) vegan margarine, plus extra for the lunchbox
pinch of sugar

For the filling
6 white asparagus spears
6 green asparagus spears
1 large or 2 small mild red chiles
10oz (300g) silken tofu
½ cup (100g) soy cream, or other plant-based cream
1 heaped tsp cornflour
1 tbsp olive oil
1 tsp dried oregano
1 tsp dried basil
freshly ground black pepper

Special equipment
11in (28cm) springform pan

Makes 2 small pizzas
Preparation: 10 minutes
+ 20 minutes rising time
+ 20 minutes cooking time

CHIA AND ALMOND PIZZA

The little superfood seeds used in this recipe guarantee a real treat for your taste buds. Instead of cheese we use almond butter with yeast flakes, which is beautifully creamy and also incredibly healthy. This gluten-free pizza with almonds will elicit a chorus of "Mmmmm!" and surpass everything you would expect from a really good pizza.

For the dough
2 tbsp ground chia seeds
1¼ cups (200g) ground almonds
½ tsp sea salt
gluten-free flour, for dusting

For the topping
⅓ cup (100g) tomato passata
2 tbsp tomato purée
½ tsp olive oil
sea salt
freshly ground white pepper
½ tsp pizza seasoning (see Tip, below)
1 small onion
½ small zucchini
1 small red pepper
1½ tbsp almond butter
1½ tsp yeast flakes
2½ cups (50g) arugula

1 To make the dough, stir the chia seeds together with 4 tbsp water and let soak for about 20 minutes. Combine the almonds and salt and knead together with the chia seeds to create a smooth dough. Preheat the oven to 400°F (200°C). Line a baking sheet with parchment paper.

2 Divide the dough in half and roll out each piece on a floured work surface using a rolling pin. Lay the discs of dough onto the baking sheet and bake in the center of the oven for 12–15 minutes until golden.

3 Meanwhile, make the sauce by stirring together the tomato passata, tomato purée, and oil, then season with salt, pepper, and pizza seasoning. Peel the onion, then slice it and the zucchini thinly. Quarter the pepper, remove the seeds, and chop into thin strips. Combine the almond butter, yeast flakes, and 3 tbsp water and stir until smooth.

4 Spread the tomato sauce on the pizza base and top with the vegetables. Dollop the almond butter mixture on top and cook the pizzas for 5–7 minutes until done. Allow to cool before packing. Pack the arugula separately. Ideally, reheat the pizza briefly before serving and garnish with the arugula.

TIP You can quickly make your own pizza seasoning from 1 tbsp each dried rosemary, oregano, basil, thyme, and yeast flakes.

Makes 1 large portion
Preparation: 55 minutes
+ 30 minutes rising time

SEMOLINA SLICE
WITH APPLE AND PEAR PURÉE

1 Peel the apples and the pear, cut into quarters, remove the core, and chop finely. Place in a saucepan with 1–2 tbsp water and bring to a boil over high heat, then cover and simmer over medium heat until the fruit is disintegrating. Lightly mash with a fork or potato masher, add sugar to taste and the cinnamon, and leave to simmer for a final 5 minutes. Set aside.

2 To make the semolina slices, bring the soy milk to a boil with the salt in a saucepan over high heat. Gradually trickle in the semolina, stirring constantly with a whisk. Simmer briefly, then transfer to a cake pan and let stand for about 30 minutes until cool.

3 Melt 1 tbsp of the margarine over medium heat in a saucepan. Cut the semolina block into pieces. Add these to the pan and dollop on the remaining margarine. Fry the slices until they are golden brown and crispy underneath; this can take up to 15 minutes. Turn and fry until crisp on the other side. Sprinkle with sugar. If desired, scatter the raisins or rum raisins over the fruit purée. Pack up the purée and semolina slices separately to take with you. Both of these also taste great cold.

For the purée
2 small apples
1 large pear
3-7 tsp brown sugar
1 tsp ground cinnamon
1 tbsp raisins or rum raisins
   (see Tip, below), for sprinkling
   (optional)

For the semolina slice
1 cup (250ml) soy milk, or other
   plant-based milk
pinch of sea salt
1 cup (150g) whole-wheat semolina
6 tbsp vegan margarine
2–3 tbsp brown sugar

Special equipment
8in (20cm) square or round cake pan

TIP

Instead of making semolina slices, you can make little balls or "dumplings." In this case, don't transfer the semolina into a pan; just remove it from the stove and allow to cool for 30 minutes. Fry the mixture in the margarine and use a fork or spoon to shape it into little balls. By the way, the apple and pear purée tastes particularly delicious with rum raisins. These are made by covering 1 tbsp raisins with rum, which you then let soak in a sealed container for 2–3 days.

SOMETHING SWEET

quick treats—creamy desserts, cakes, & pastries

FRUITY
MACADAMIA CREAM

Mellow vanilla seeds enhance this exquisite dessert that is prepared using macadamia nuts, puréed with succulent zucchini, orange juice, and maple syrup until creamy. Served with vitamin-rich fresh berries and vegan white chocolate, this is a feast for the eyes and the mouth.

7oz (200g) macadamia nuts
1 small zucchini
3½ tbsp apple juice (optional)
scant 1oz (25g) goji berries
   (optional)
2–3 tbsp orange juice
4–5 tbsp maple syrup
scraped-out seeds from
   ½ vanilla pod
pinch of salt
⅓ cup (50g) blueberries
⅓ cup (50g) raspberries
a few mint leaves (optional)
1¾oz (50g) vegan white chocolate

1 Soak the macadamia nuts in cold water for 12 hours. Peel the zucchini, slice in half lengthwise, and remove the seeds. Chop the remaining vegetable into coarse chunks. Bring the apple juice to a boil and add the goji berries (if using), then remove the pan from the stove and set aside.

2 Purée the macadamias, zucchini, orange juice, maple syrup, vanilla seeds, and salt in a food processor until you have a smooth, creamy consistency. Drain the goji berries in a colander and fold into the cream. Transfer the cream into 2 containers or jars with lids.

3 Scatter the blueberries, raspberries, and mint (if using) on top of the cream, then grate over the chocolate. Seal the containers and store in the fridge until ready for eating or transporting.

TIP For an even more chocolatey touch, add ½ cup (50g) cocoa powder to the cream.

CHIA AND CASHEW PUDDING
WITH APRICOT PURÉE

Healthy chia seeds are a quick and easy way to transform cashew cream into an excellent dessert. A sweet apricot purée adds a fruity finishing touch. If you also include some acai fruit powder, you are guaranteed a really nourishing snack.

1 To make the pudding, put all the ingredients except for the chia seeds into a food processor and purée until you have a smooth cashew cream. Add the chia seeds and 1 cup (250ml) water and stir well. Transfer the mixture to a screw-top jar or other sealable container and let stand for at least 20 minutes in the fridge so that the chia seeds can swell.

2 Meanwhile, halve the apricots lengthwise and remove the pits. Finely purée the apricots with the maple syrup in a food processor. Stir in the acai berry powder right away (if using), or sprinkle it over the purée later as decoration.

3 Top the chia cashew dessert with the apricot purée and garnish with acai berry powder (if using) if you chose not to stir it into the purée in the previous step. Seal the containers and store in the fridge until ready to eat or transport.

For the pudding
1 tbsp cocoa powder
4 pitted dates
1 tbsp cashew nut butter
1 tsp agave syrup
finely grated zest of 1 small
   unwaxed orange
3 tbsp chia seeds

For the purée
5½oz (150g) apricots
1 tsp maple syrup
1 heaped tsp acai berry powder
   (from a health food store,
   optional)

2 cups (500ml) rice milk
1 tsp vanilla sugar, or ½ tsp pure
    vanilla extract
pinch of sea salt
½ cup (125g) pudding rice
whole-wheat breadcrumbs, for
    the pan
¼ cup (50g) granulated sugar
½ tsp ground cinnamon
2 tbsp vegan margarine
3 cups (420g) strawberries

Special equipment
8in (20cm) cake pan

CARAMELIZED RICE PUDDING CAKES WITH STRAWBERRIES

1 To make the rice, stir the rice milk in a saucepan over medium heat with the vanilla sugar or extract and salt and bring to a boil. Reduce the heat, gradually pour in the pudding rice, stirring constantly, and simmer for 10 minutes. Sprinkle an 8in (20cm) cake pan with breadcrumbs and pour the rice into the pan so it forms a layer about 1½in (4cm) thick. Allow to cool, cover with plastic wrap, and chill in the fridge for at least 12 hours.

2 Turn the rice out of the pan and chop into pieces. Mix the sugar and cinnamon on a plate and press the pieces into the mix on both sides. Melt the margarine in a pan over medium heat and fry the rice slices on both sides until the sugar has caramelized. Let cool slightly, and transfer to your lunchbox. Pack up the strawberries separately to take with you.

2 medium-tart apples
juice of 1 small lemon
½ cup (150g) coconut cream
scraped-out seeds from
    ½ vanilla pod
1 tbsp maple syrup
¼ cup (50g) puffed whole-grain
    quinoa
½ cup (60g) aronia berries (sweet
    and sour berries), or blueberries
1 tbsp hazelnut brittle

FALL APPLE DREAM

1 Peel, quarter, and core the apples, then grate coarsely into a bowl. Drizzle the apple with lemon juice. Beat the cream and fold into the fruit along with the vanilla seeds and maple syrup.

2 Layer up the apple cream mixture alternately with puffed quinoa and aronia berries in a screw-top jar. Finish with an apple and cream layer and sprinkle with hazelnut brittle. Seal the jars or containers and chill until ready to eat or transport.

TIP For an (even) easier treat, use coconut yogurt or soy yogurt instead of the cream.

Makes 10–12 pieces
Preparation: 25 minutes
+ 30 minutes cooking time
+ 12 hours resting time

BAKLAVA

This tempting exotic delicacy with walnuts and pistachios is available all over the world, so naturally our lunchbox couldn't be without it. We all know how sweet things lift your spirits, so why not bring a bit of joy to your lunch breaks? While you're at it, pack up some extra portions of this vegan treat and spread a bit of happiness among your coworkers, too.

1 To make the syrup, bring 2 cups of water and the sugar to a boil in a saucepan. Stir in the lemon juice and remove the pan from the heat. Preheat the oven to 400°F (200°C). For the filling, melt the margarine in a small pan over low heat. Then, finely chop the walnuts and pistachios and mix with the cinnamon.

2 Grease a baking sheet. Lay a pastry sheet on the sheet and brush with some melted margarine. Loosely lay another sheet on top and scatter some of the chopped nuts evenly over it. Continue layering pastry and nuts in this way, brushing with margarine (reserving 1–2 tbsp), and finishing with an upper layer of pastry. Press together the pastry edges so the filling cannot leak out. Cut into rectangles about 1½ × ¾in (4 × 2cm) and brush with the reserved margarine.

3 Bake the baklava in the center of the oven for around 30 minutes until golden brown. Remove from the oven and spoon the syrup evenly over, allowing it time to absorb until you have used it all. Let stand for about 12 hours.

1¾ cups (350g) granulated sugar
juice of ½ small lemon
½ cup (125g) vegan margarine, plus extra for the baking sheet
7oz (200g) walnuts
3½oz (100g) pistachios
1 tsp ground cinnamon
8oz (225g) yufka pastry sheets (from a Turkish store, or online), or filo pastry

TIP

Baklava will keep for 2 weeks in a well-sealed container. Don't store the pieces on top of each other!

Makes 6
Preparation: 25 minutes
+ 100 minutes rising time
+ 20 minutes cooking time

EASTER BUNS

Traditional Austrian yeasted buns (*pinzen*) have inspired this recipe for particularly handy lunchbox sweet rolls. The deliciously light dough contains rum-flavored raisins and is finished off with an apricot jam glaze, scattered with pearl sugar. Traditionally, the buns are eaten at Easter...but something this delicious deserves to be enjoyed throughout the year.

4 cups (500g) flour, plus extra
  for dusting
1½ tsp finely grated unwaxed
  lemon zest
pinch of sea salt
5 tbsp vegan margarine
¾oz (20g) fresh yeast
½ cup (80g) granulated sugar
2 tsp vanilla sugar, or 1 tsp pure
  vanilla extract
1 cup (260ml) soy milk, or other
  plant-based milk, plus extra
  for brushing
¾ cup (100g) rum raisins (see p161)
2–3 tbsp apricot jam
pearl sugar, for sprinkling

1 Mix the flour, lemon zest, and salt in a bowl. Add the margarine in little spoonfuls and work it in using your fingertips. Create a dip in the mix, crumble in the yeast, and add both the sugar and the vanilla sugar or pure vanilla extract. Warm the soy milk in a pan over low heat and pour it in. Dust with some flour and leave this starter mix, covered, in a warm place for about 10 minutes to rise.

2 Add the rum raisins to the starter mix and knead everything for 10 minutes until you have a smooth, yeasty dough. If the dough is too moist, add a bit of flour—but take care to make sure the dough doesn't become too firm. Cover and let rise in a warm place for 1 hour.

3 Preheat the oven to 350°F (180°C). Line a baking sheet with parchment paper. Knead the dough briefly once again on a floured work surface and divide it into 6 portions. Shape each piece into a long, thick sausage, lay it on the baking sheet, and allow to rise for 30 minutes.

4 Snip into the buns several times (see photo). Brush with soy milk and bake in the center of the oven for 18–20 minutes. Remove from the oven, transfer to a wire rack to cool, brush with the apricot jam, and sprinkle with pearl sugar.

PEANUT BUTTER AND PUFFED RICE CRISPIES

Makes 10–12
Preparation: 10 minutes
+ 12 hours chilling time

In a bowl, stir together the peanut butter, margarine, cinnamon, and agave syrup until smooth. Stir in the puffed rice until evenly distributed. Chill for around 15 minutes, then use your hands to form 10–12 little balls from the mixture. Transfer the balls to a well-sealed container and allow to rest for around 12 hours in the fridge, to set fully.

4 tbsp soft, slightly salted crunchy peanut butter
1 tbsp soft vegan margarine
½ tsp ground cinnamon
1½ tbsp agave syrup
1 cup (15g) puffed rice

REDCURRANT AND COCONUT TURNOVERS

Makes 5
Preparation: 25 minutes
+ 15 minutes cooking time

1 Preheat the oven to 425°F (220°C). Line a baking sheet with parchment paper. Combine the flour, sugar, baking powder, baking soda, desiccated coconut, and salt in a bowl using a whisk. Stir together the soy milk and lemon juice and let stand for 5 minutes. Meanwhile, remove the stalks from the redcurrants. Stir the lemon zest into the milk and juice mixture and add this to the flour mixture with the margarine. Knead everything together until you have a smooth dough.

2 Roll out the dough on a floured work surface to create a large rectangle measuring about 12 × 11in (30 × 28cm). Spread the redcurrants evenly across half the dough sheet and fold the other half over, pressing the edges together. Slice the filled pastry slab into 5 equal-sized triangles. Press the dough firmly together again at the edges. Lay the turnovers on the baking sheet and bake in the center of the oven for around 15 minutes until they are light brown on top. Let cool on a wire rack.

3 Make the glaze (if using) by cooking the redcurrants in a small saucepan with 1 tbsp water until the berries pop open. Press them through a strainer. Sift the powdered sugar into a bowl and stir in the redcurrant juice until smooth. Brush the pockets with the glaze and sprinkle with desiccated coconut or coconut flakes.

For the pockets
2½ cups (300g) white spelt flour, plus extra for dusting
½ cup (100g) granulated sugar
1 tsp baking powder
¾ tsp baking soda
⅓ cup (30g) dried coconut
pinch of sea salt
½ cup (100ml) soy milk, or other plant-based milk
1 tsp lemon juice
1⅓ cups (150g) redcurrants
finely grated zest of 1 unwaxed lemon
4 tbsp soft vegan margarine

For the glaze (optional)
½ cup (50g) redcurrants
1¼ cups (150g) powdered sugar
dried coconut or coconut flakes, for sprinkling

JUICY MANDARIN AND CHIA SEED MUFFINS

These fruity muffins will really sweeten up your office! They are a handy size and the mandarins give them a truly indulgent juicy sweetness which is rounded off perfectly by the combination of wheat and nutty spelt flours.

⅓ cup (50g) bread flour
½ cup (75g) all-purpose flour
3 tbsp whole-wheat spelt flour
½ tsp baking soda
¾ tsp baking powder
1 tsp chia seeds
⅓ cup (75g) granulated sugar
½ cup (125g) soy yogurt, or other plant-based yogurt
2 tbsp soy milk, or other plant-based milk
1 tbsp agave syrup
2 tbsp oil
½ tsp edible mandarin oil (from a health food store or online, optional)
juice and grated zest of 2 unwaxed mandarins

1 Preheat the oven to 350°F (180°C). Put 6 paper liners into a muffin pan. Mix together the 3 types of flour, baking soda, baking powder, chia seeds, and sugar in a bowl with a whisk.

2 In another bowl, whisk the yogurt with the milk, agave syrup, oil, and mandarin oil (if using). Stir in the mandarin juice and zest. Add the yogurt mixture to the flour mixture and combine everything with a spoon, just until all the ingredients are combined and you have a smooth mixture.

3 Distribute the mixture between the muffin cups so that they are each around two-thirds full. Bake the muffins in the center of the oven for around 25 minutes until golden. Insert a wooden toothpick: if no mixture sticks to it, the muffins are done. (Otherwise, continue to cook for a couple more minutes, then test again.) Lift the muffins in their liners out of the pan and allow to cool on a wire rack.

Makes 10
Preparation: 35 minutes
+ 2 hours rising time
+ 20 minutes cooking time

CINNAMON SWIRLS
WITH CASHEW MAPLE
ICING AND PECANS

1 For the icing, cover the cashews with cold water to soak. To make the dough, mix both types of flour, the sugar, yeast, salt, and nutmeg in a bowl with a whisk. Heat the applesauce, soy milk, and margarine in a saucepan over low heat and stir. Remove the pan from the heat and leave the apple mixture to cool. Add the apple mixture to the flour mixture and knead everything for 10 minutes, until you have a smooth and supple dough. Cover and let the dough rise in a warm place for 1 hour, 30 minutes.

2 Knead the dough briefly once again on a floured work surface and roll it out to create a rectangle. For the filling, melt the margarine in a small pan over medium heat. Stir in both types of sugar and the cinnamon and spread the mixture evenly over the dough. Roll up the dough from a long edge and cut the roll into 2in (5cm) thick slices. Line a baking sheet with parchment paper. Gently press the dough swirls flat, lay them on the baking sheet, cover, and let rise for another 30 minutes.

3 Preheat the oven to 350°F (180°C). Brush the dough with soy milk and bake in the center of the oven for 18–20 minutes. Remove from the oven and allow to cool.

4 To make the caramelized pecans, let the sugar and 2½ tbsp water gently caramelize in a pan over medium heat. Stir in the pecans, transfer the mixture to a piece of parchment paper, and allow to cool. Finely chop the nuts with a large sharp knife.

5 Drain the cashews in a colander. Pulse them in a food processor with some maple syrup until smooth, adding a splash of water if required. Spread the cashew icing on the cinnamon swirls and sprinkle with chopped caramelized pecans.

For the icing and pecans
7oz (200g) cashews
⅓ cup (50g) demerara sugar
3½oz (100g) pecans
maple syrup

For the dough
2½ cups (300g) all-purpose flour,
  plus extra for dusting
1¼ cups (150g) whole-wheat spelt flour
3 tbsp granulated sugar
¼oz (7g) packet of dried yeast
1 tsp sea salt
pinch of freshly grated nutmeg
½ cup (140g) applesauce
⅔ cup (150ml) soy milk, or other
  plant-based milk, plus extra
  for brushing
⅓ cup (80g) vegan margarine

For the filling
¼ cup (60g) vegan margarine
½ cup (60g) brown sugar
⅓ cup (60g) granulated sugar
3 slightly heaped tsp
  ground cinnamon

**Makes a 9½in (24cm) tart/
12 pieces**
Preparation: 40 minutes
+ 50 minutes rising time
+ 45 minutes cooking time

RASPBERRY AND CHOCOLATE "WINDMILL"

For the dough
3½ cups (450g) all-purpose flour,
    plus extra for dusting
3 tsp cocoa powder
pinch of sea salt
½ tsp finely grated zest of
    1 unwaxed lemon
1 cup (180g) granulated sugar
⅓ cup (70g) soft vegan margarine,
    plus more for the pan
1 cup (220ml) soy milk, or other
    plant-based milk
¾oz (20g) fresh yeast

For the custard
1⅔ cups (380ml) soy milk, or other
    plant-based milk
¼ cup (50g) granulated sugar
3oz (75g) package of vegan vanilla
    custard powder

For the filling
2oz (60g) vegan dark chocolate
2 cups (250g) raspberries
2½ tbsp cornflour
2½ tbsp confectioner's sugar

For the decoration (optional)
1¾oz (50g) vegan dark chocolate
1 tsp coconut oil
½ cup (50g) raspberries

Special equipment
9½in (24cm) springform pan

1 To make the dough, mix the flour, cocoa powder, salt, lemon zest, and half the sugar in a bowl using a whisk. Add blobs of margarine and rub it in with your fingers. Make a dip in the center of the mix. Heat the soy milk in a pan over low heat, pour it into the dip, and crumble in the yeast. Sprinkle the remaining sugar over the milk and yeast mixture and dust with a bit of flour. Cover and allow this starter mix to rise in a warm place for around 10 minutes. Stir once again and knead for 10 minutes until you have a smooth dough. Cover and let rise in a warm place for 40 minutes.

2 Meanwhile, make the custard by bringing half the soy milk to a boil with the sugar in a pan over high heat. Stir the custard powder into the remaining milk until smooth. As soon as the milk boils, remove the pan from the heat and add the custard powder and milk mixture, stirring constantly. Return the pan to the heat and bring everything to a boil once again, continuing to stir all the time. Remove from the heat and allow to cool. Give it a stir every so often to prevent a skin from forming.

3 Grease a 9½in (24cm) springform pan. Roughly chop the chocolate for the filling. Roll out the dough on a floured work surface to form a rectangle measuring about 16 × 12in (40 × 30cm). Spread the vanilla custard over the dough and then sprinkle over the chocolate chunks and raspberries. Mix together the cornflour and confectioner's sugar and sift over.

4 Preheat the oven to 350°F (180°C). Cut the slab of dough into 1½in (4cm) wide strips. Roll one of the strips into a snail shape and place this in the center of the pan. Arrange the other strips around it, working out in a spiral toward the edge of the pan. Bake in the center of the oven for 40–45 minutes. If it looks too dark after 15 minutes, cover with a sheet of parchment paper. Remove and allow to cool on a wire rack.

5 Chop the chocolate for decorating (if using), and melt it with the coconut oil in a ovenproof bowl suspended over a saucepan of simmering water. Stir well. Decorate the cake with the melted chocolate and raspberries.

Makes 1 large braid
Preparation: 30 minutes
+ 100 minutes rising time
+ 35 minutes cooking time

TRIPLE NUT BRAID

Walnuts, almonds, and hazelnuts make a fabulous combination in this yeasted braid. It tastes better than anything you could buy from a bakery, not to mention the fact it's made without any animal products. Homemade is always best—just sit back and enjoy the results!

For the dough

4 cups (500g) all-purpose flour, plus extra for dusting

½ tsp sea salt

5 tbsp soft vegan margarine, plus extra for the baking sheet

¾oz (20g) fresh yeast

½ cup (80g) granulated sugar

1 tsp vanilla sugar, or ½ tsp pure vanilla extract

1½ cups (260ml) almond milk, or other plant-based milk

For the filling

3½oz (100g) ground walnuts

3½oz (100g) ground almonds

3½oz (100g) ground hazelnuts

3 heaped tbsp whole-wheat breadcrumbs

2 tbsp vegan margarine

8 tbsp agave syrup

2 tbsp vanilla sugar, or 2 tsp pure vanilla extract

½ tsp ground cinnamon

1 cup (220ml) almond milk, or other plant-based milk

½ cup (200g) apricot jam

1 To make the dough, mix the flour and salt in a bowl. Add spoonfuls of margarine and rub in with your fingers. Make a dip in the mix, crumble in the yeast, and sprinkle over the granulated sugar and vanilla sugar or extract. Heat the almond milk in a pan over low heat and pour it in. Dust with a bit of flour, cover, and let this mix rise in a warm place for around 10 minutes. Knead for 10 minutes to create a smooth dough. Cover and let rise at room temperature for at least 1 hour. Knead it through once again and let rise for 30 minutes more.

2 Meanwhile, mix the walnuts, almonds, hazelnuts, and breadcrumbs for the filling in a bowl. Put the margarine into a large pan with the agave syrup, vanilla sugar or extract, cinnamon, and almond milk and bring to a boil, then stir well over medium heat. Stir in the nut mixture and remove the pan from the heat.

3 Preheat the oven to 350°F (180°C). Grease a baking sheet. Roll out the dough to create a ¼in (5mm) thick rectangle. Spread the jam evenly over it and top with the nut filling. Roll up the dough from a long edge and press together gently. Cut the roll lengthwise through the center either once or twice, then twist each piece so that the cut edges face upward. Either intertwine the dough pieces into a "cord" or braid them. Lay the braid on the baking sheet and bake in the center of the oven for 30–35 minutes until golden brown. Remove from the sheet and let cool on a wire rack.

Makes a 8in (20cm) loaf cake
Preparation: 30 minutes
+ 50 minutes cooking time

SUPER-CHOCOLATEY SNACKING CAKE

This loaf cake certainly deserves its name! It contains not only cocoa powder, but also chocolate chips, and two further types of melted chocolate poured on top. Because one thing is clear: chocolate makes you really happy. It's definitely good for a slow Wednesday at work.

For the cake
vegan margarine, for the pan
1¼ cups (150g) all-purpose flour, plus extra for the pan
1 cup (100g) white spelt flour
½ cup (130g) granulated sugar
1 tbsp vanilla sugar, or 1½ tsp pure vanilla extract
1½ tsp baking soda
½ cup (40g) cocoa powder
2oz (60g) vegan dark chocolate, chopped
4 tbsp soy milk, or other plant-based milk
2 tsp white wine vinegar
4 tbsp vegetable oil
1 cup (220ml) carbonated mineral water

For the frosting
2oz (60g) vegan dark chocolate
1 tbsp soy cream, or other plant-based cream
¾oz (20g) vegan white chocolate

Special equipment
8in (20cm) long loaf pan

1 Preheat the oven to 350°F (180°C). Grease the loaf pan with margarine and dust with flour. Combine both types of flour, the granulated sugar, vanilla sugar or extract, baking soda, and cocoa powder in a bowl with a whisk.

2 In a separate bowl, stir together the soy milk and vinegar, let stand for 10 minutes, then stir in the oil. Add the soy milk mixture to the flour mixture, then pour in the mineral water, mixing everything swiftly but delicately with a spoon to create a smooth consistency. Fold in the chopped chocolate. Immediately transfer the mixture to a 8in (20cm) long loaf pan and bake in the center of the oven for 50 minutes. Remove and allow to cool on a wire rack.

3 To make the frosting, chop the dark chocolate, add it to a heavy-bottomed saucepan with the cream, and let it melt over low heat. Frost the cake with this mixture and let it dry. Melt the white chocolate in a ovenproof bowl over a saucepan of simmering water. Transfer it to a freezer bag, carefully snip off a corner and, with swift movements, draw decorative lines across the cake. Let set, then slice and pack up to take with you.

BUCKWHEAT PANCAKES
WITH CARAMELIZED APPLE SLICES

The gluten-free batter for these pancakes is made from hearty buckwheat flour.
The apple lends sweetness and moisture and it caramelizes really beautifully
in the pan. You could also make a savory version (see Tip, below).

1 Mix together the flour, baking powder, vanilla seeds, sugar, and
salt in a bowl. Add the mineral water and stir everything until you
have a smooth consistency. Peel, quarter, and core the apple, then
slice thinly. Place the apple slices in a small bowl of water with the
lemon juice.

2 Heat half the oil in the pan, add half the batter, spreading
it out slightly if necessary, and top with half the apple slices.
Cook over medium heat until the edges are firm. Sprinkle over
half the sugar. Turn the pancake and cook the other side until it is
also golden brown, then remove from the pan. Cook the second
pancake in the same way using the remaining ingredients. Allow
to cool, then package up to take with you. Tastes great either
warm or cold.

1 cup (125g) buckwheat flour
1 tsp baking powder
scraped-out seeds from
    ¼ vanilla pod
1 tbsp granulated sugar
pinch of sea salt
1¼ cups (300ml) ice-cold
    carbonated mineral water
1 tart apple
juice of ½ lemon
3 tbsp flavorless vegetable oil
8 tsp brown sugar

TIP

The apple slices can also be served separately
from the pancakes. Alternatively, for a savory
meal, prepare the pancakes with your choice
of chopped onion, vegetables (pepper pieces,
sweetcorn), salt, or fresh herbs.

INDEX

THE AUTHORS ...

After training as a chef and food technician, Jérôme Eckmeier worked in numerous prestigious restaurants in Germany and abroad. He has been cooking vegan food and following a vegan diet for many years. He regularly conjures up inspirational new vegan dishes in his online cooking show and his blog.

I would like to thank my wife Melanie (for being so patient with me), our children, and my parents. Thanks also go out to: Franz and Traute, Marius and Frauke, the Keller family, Dr. Norbert Knitsch, the Eckmeier clan from the Ruhr region, the guys at Budo Nüttermoor, my sensei Hardwig Tomic, Markus from Little Harbour Tattoo, the German Vegetarian Society [VEBU], Bernd Drosihn from tofutown, Sebastian Bete from the OZ [Ostfriesen-Zeitung: German regional newspaper], Erwin and Sandra, Ingo Jäger, Tatjana and Boris Seifert, Brigitte "the sun" Kelly, Nicole Bader, Andreas Kessemeier and the staff at Pool Position, Mike Beuger at the law firm WBS in Cologne, Vik and Tina, the team at VHS Leer [adult education center], Vegetarisch Fit [German magazine: Healthy Vegetarian], cinemadirekt Berlin, Keimling Naturkost [health food shop], Jan Bredack and his family, the team at Veganz, Baola Munich, Chris at myey.info, Roadhouse Herbrum, and all those folks and rock 'n' roll types who support my work.

Photo: © Boris Seifert

Jérôme
Eckmeier

Daniela Lais worked as a freelance journalist for more than a decade and currently works for the vegan bakery at the long-established vegetarian/vegan restaurant Ginko in Graz. She has been vegan for more than ten years and incorporates this lifestyle into her work and travel, too.

I would like to thank my partner Michael for being a much-appreciated food taster for this book and for always offering his supportive and honest opinion. Thanks also go to my parents and all those friends who have enjoyed my creations and offered me support. Thanks to my American friends Janet, Steven, and Denise who have inspired me to create so many recipes and who continually encourage me to fulfill my ideas and dreams. Thanks to my dog Lilly, who enriches my life in so many ways. Special thanks also go to my publisher DK, especially to Sarah Fischer, who worked with such enthusiasm to help me create my perfect book. To Sabine Durdel-Hoffmann, Brigitte Sporrer, for the fantastic photography, to Jérôme Eckmeier and the German Vegetarian Society [VEBU]. I would also like to thank my bakery colleagues in Graz, particularly Franziska Gregor, who has been such a role model for me as an individual, as an animal rights activist, and as a baker. Thank you to all those people who are committed to animal welfare and animal rights, to my coffee providers who keep me alert and functioning with a constant supply of great coffee, and to all those people who support me on my journey through life.

Photo: personal

Daniela
Lais

Photography Brigitte Sporrer
Food styling Julia Skowronek
Design Sonja Gagel
Editors Sabine Durdel-Hoffmann and Karin Kerber

For DK Germany:
Publisher Monika Schlitzer
Senior editor Caren Hummel
Project editor Sarah Fischer
Producer Dorothee Whittaker
Production coordinator Arnika Marx
Production Christine Rühmer

For DK UK:
Editor Lucy Bannell
Translator Alison Tunley
Senior editor Kathryn Meeker
Senior art editor Glenda Fisher
Jacket designer Steve Marsden
Producer, pre-production Catherine Williams
Producer Stephanie McConnell
Creative technical support Sonia Charbonnier
Managing editor Stephanie Farrow
Managing art editor Christine Keilty
US editor Kayla Dugger
Americanizer Jenny Siklos

First American Edition, 2017
Published in the United States by DK Publishing
345 Hudson Street, New York, New York 10014

A catalog record for this book is available from the Library of Congress.
ISBN 978-1-4654-6183-4

DK books are available at special discounts when purchased in bulk for sales promotions, premiums,
fund-raising, or educational use. For details, contact: DK Publishing Special
Markets, 345 Hudson Street, New York, New York 10014 SpecialSales@dk.com

Printed and bound in China

A WORLD OF IDEAS:
SEE ALL THERE IS TO KNOW
www.dk.com